SOUS VIDE COOKBOOK

Your Ultimate Guide to Quick & Easy Days of Sous Vide Cooking

By
ESTELLA
FRANCO

Table of Contents

Introduction

Regardless of whatever people might say, there is a hidden "Want" inside all of us to be able to create the most wonderful and magical meals that would help to win the heart of your family members and loved ones. However, this is a feeble dream for some individuals who aren't blessed with the art of cooking and aren't able to manage enough time to hone their skill! There was a time when even I was unable to cook an Omelet properly.

If you fall under that particular category, then you might be wondering now, is this the end of your culinary dreams? Well of course not! Thanks to constant evolutions in culinary technologies, we have amazing devices that not only make our cooking life easier but also makes it much more accessible so that anyone can cook wonderful meals, even without having an in-depth experience! While it is true that there are some amazing appliances to consider such as the Air Fryer, Instant Pot, and Crock Pot etc., an undeniable fact is that the Sous Vide Appliances stand on a league of its own!

Best part about Sous Vide

You will be able to cook perfect meal every single time, regardless of your culinary skill levels! It might sound a little bit hard to believe, but it's true! Before letting you go wild into the 100+ amazing recipes, which you can find in this book, I would like you to go through this introductory chapter to know more about your shiny Sous Vide device!

If you are already an experienced veteran, hope you will find some interesting things throughout the reading. Alternatively, if you are an amateur and interested in learning the craft, the brief introductory chapter will give you all the necessary information required to help you fully grasp the science behind Sous Vide cooking.

Chapter 1: What Is Sous Vide?

The term sous vide is a French term, which loosely translates to "under vacuum".

That's why you can think of it as the process of vacuum sealing food in an airtight bag then cooking it in a water bath to a very precise temperature. Although the term Sous Vide sounds exotic and hard to understand, we use it describe the vacuum culinary technique. This method brings ingredients and spices together in a heat-proof bag and cooks in a water bath at a steady temperature. Because the temperatures are lower than the temperatures other cooking method uses, the cooking process is very long and can take around 10 hours, for some thicker cuts of meat.

Sous Vide technique is developing for centuries. This is the best method you can use to prepare foods that lose their quality when made with classic cooking methods. A good example is an octopus, chewy, or tough meat. This technique will preserve all their qualities while making them tender and perfect for consumption. Besides mentioned, Sous Vide has other advantages over classic culinary methods.

While the traditional methods can dry out or burn food, with the Sous Vide, you can forget these mistakes. This technique will always offer a well-cooked, juicy, and flavor-intensive dish.

The Sous Vide method is perfect for the preparation of meat and seafood. When you fry a fish fillet, the skillet reaches up to 400F. This temperature is far away from the ideal center temperature of the fish. This results in overcooked edges and sometimes raw center. The term "Sous Vide" is French for "cooking in a vacuum." Still, the main characteristic of this cooking method is not the package, but precision temperature. Intelligent heaters can heat up water to the desired temperature, and most importantly keep it at that temperature for hours. With this method, you can relax and continue with your chores, whether in the kitchen or around the house. This is something you cannot do when baking in the oven or frying in the fryer. One second of being reckless can cost you lunch.

The History Of Sous Vide

So, how did the idea of cooking food in vacuum-sealed bags come about?

Benjamin Thompson, Count Rumford was the first to describe low temperature cooking in 1799. He placed a shoulder of mutton in a machine he had invented to roast potatoes. As he was attempting to see whether he could roast meat, Benjamin used air as the medium of heat transfer in his experiments. He cooked the meat for 3 hours after which he gave up and gave the meat to the maids. With the intention of cooking the meat the next day, the maids left it in the machine only to wake up the next day and discover that the meat was fully cooked and perfectly done. In his own words, Benjamin described the meat as

In the mid-1960s, preparing foods under pressure with or without heat was discovered by French and American engineers. The researchers observed that cooking using this method, the resulting food showed distinctive improvements with texture and flavor. While this method began to develop, vacuum sealing was sometimes referred to as "cryovacking". Even without cooking, the pressure notably improved the concentration of the fruits' flavors. In 1974, George Pralus, a French chef adopted the method for the restaurant Troisgros (of Michel and Pierre Troisgros) in Roanne, France. He observed that when foie gras was cooked using this method, it had better texture, did not lose excess amounts of fat and kept its original appearance.

Bruno Goussault, the Chief scientist at Sterling, Virginia, was another pioneer in sous vide. He was the top food manufacturer of Cuisine Solutions who did further research of how temperature affects different types of foods. He was later well known for training top chefs in this method and developing parameters of cooking temperature and times for various foods. In the 1970s, Bruno and George worked independently on the development of sous vide and eventually became collaborators. Bruno was the one who pioneered the union of low temperature cooking and vacuum sealing and thus sous vide was born. George is considered to be the pioneer of modern sous vide where cooking takes place at fairly high temperatures.

*Note: The results produced by using this technique are impossible to achieve using any other cooking method, as it cooks food to the exact desired level of doneness every time. I know you might be wondering; why go through the trouble of cooking your food this way? The benefits of Sous Vide cooking that we will discuss next will amaze you:

Why Go Through the Trouble to Use Sous Vide Cooking?

1: Helps you organize your cooking time

This is one of the greatest things about sous vide cooking; that it gives you more control over your cooking times. You can prepare your food and vacuum seal it up to a day in advance and leave it to cook slowly in the water oven. It also gives you the pleasure of coming back and serving up your meal whenever you are ready to eat. The best part is that you can even sous vide overnight.

2: No more burnt, chewy or undercooked food

It is not uncommon to end up with food where a piece is cooked on the outside but still raw on the inside when pan- frying. In such instances, cooking the food until it is very well done on the inside means that the outside can easily end up overcooked or even burnt. This problem never arises with sous vide cooking where the food cooks evenly all the way through at a low temperature and can be later on seared or browned.

It is nearly impossible to overcook food in a water bath.

3: Great quality delicious food

Sous vide cooked food is utterly delicious and infinitely more appealing, the reason being that since the food is placed in a vacuum sealed bag, it does not lose its form or dehydrate while cooking. The original flavor, weight, aroma and natural color of the food is not lost. It also means that you can utilize forgotten or cheaper cuts of meat to your advantage. Other than that, sous vide produces food in the texture that it is meant to be eaten. Gone are the days of soggy asparagus and chewy chicken – sous vide vegetables retain their color and crunch and the meat is moist and tender.

4: Healthier food

As mentioned above, foods cooked through sous vide retain their flavors; therefore, little or no additional fat or salt is required during cooking. In addition, cooking food in a vacuum sealed bag means that the minerals and vitamins are not lost during the process unlike in steaming or boiling.

5: Consistent good results

You can prepare the same dish repeatedly while achieving the exact same results with the extremely precise temperature control of sous vide cooking.

6: It is simpler and quicker to prepare meals

Using the sous vide water bath is pretty much just as easy as using any slow cooker. Once you have prepared your food for cooking (which sometimes could be as easy as packing steak into a vacuum sealed bag), it is as easy as just placing the bag in the water bath once it reaches the right temperature. Most meals can be prepared and cooked with less than 30 minutes.

If you are new to all this, I know you might be wondering how this cooking method came into being. Let's discuss that. From the above discussion, it is clear that you need special cooking appliances for sous vide cooking. Let's discuss that next to prepare you for the next level of cooking:

Sous Vide Appliances

There are a variety of sous vide appliances but it is easier for you to choose one based on the affordability, ease of use, energy required, purpose, efficiency and such.

Sous Vide Supreme Demi Water Oven

Why buy it: If you are planning to do a lot of sous vide cooking, you will appreciate this machine because it is made of quality materials and can hold lots of food.

Who it's for: Anyone wanting an ultra-high quality and reliable countertop sous vide machine?

Cost: $342

This machine brings sous vide cooking closer to home cooks. It is almost the size of a crockpot (measuring 29cm x 28cm x 33cm) and can be store easily in a cabinet or a countertop. It's a high-quality water oven yet affordable enough for non- commercial use.

The demi water oven has a steam containing lid and double walled insulation, so no steam escapes and its cool to touch on the outside. It can hold water at your desired temp for several days and the timer can be set for up to 99 hours. It can maintain the temperature of water between 86- and 210- degrees F within 1-degree accuracy.

The machine is completely quiet, as it does not run on a motor. It has a perforated bottom grill, which allows it to generate thermal turbulence. The water capacity of the water bath is 2.3 gallons, so it can hold quite a bit of food —up to 12 pouches of 4 Oz. each of food. It comes with a stainless-steel rack for the correct positioning of food.

The major limitation of this machine is the price. It is quite expensive at $342.

Anova precision cooker nano

Why buy it: This is an ideal option if you want to give sous vide a try without spending a ton of cash

Who it's for: Anyone in search of a sous vide machine that does not require a lot of space

Cost: $65 to $99

This is quite a well-known brand of sous vide. It can be attached virtually to any pot that is large enough to hold your desired water capacity and ingredients. It can heat 5 gallons of water to 32- and 197-degrees F.

One major issue with this machine is the lack of accuracy; maintaining the perfect water bath temperature is vital. It maintains water bath temperature within a range of 0.1 degrees F.

One cool feature of the device is that it has a Bluetooth app (BLE 4.2), which gives you the ability to control the machine remotely with your phone. The app also has easy-to-follow recipes that only require the push of a button to start – you can also use the app to create your own recipes.

The major drawbacks of this machine is that the clamp does not open wide enough and that it is not as powerful as other sous vide machines so don't overload the water bath.

Anova precision cooker Wi-Fi

Why buy it: It is great for just about anyone (its user friendly) whether you are a professional chef or an amateur.

Who it's for: Anyone who wants the pleasure of controlling their sous vide machine with voice or an app.

<u>*Cost: $90 to $199.*</u>

This machine clamps onto the side of your cooking pot without the need of a magnetic base. It requires you to fiddle with it for a few seconds but once in place, it is secure. It allows you to control it with your tablet, Smartphone or smart home devices such as Google home and Alexa.

It also features an LED backlit scroll wheel and LCD display for users who do not want to control it externally.

The anova precision cooker is a good choice for you if you want the flexibility to cook your meal with additional precisions or without them.

The maximum capacity as per the manufacturer's recommendations is 4 to 5 gallons.

CHEFSTEPS CS10001 JOULE SOUS VIDE

Why buy it: You can control it with your voice or a Smartphone app and it cooks the perfect steak.

Who it's for: Anyone who wants a small device that makes easy, restaurant quality meals at home. Also, if you desire a smart kitchen and the ability to control your cooking device with apps, you will like this.

Cost: $199

This is the best sous vide appliance. It has great integration, power, speed and durability. It is made out of stainless steel and extruded polycarbonate, which gives it added durability and strength. It also has a magnetic base, which allows it to stick to your pot without the need of a clamp.

The Joule rises above and sets trends when it comes to integration. You can connect this devices immersion circulator to your tablet or Smartphone and use its visual tool to choose the way you want your steak to look once you are done cooking it. When you have raw meat that needs some cooking, you can even connect this machine to Facebook messenger or Alexa and just say "Joule, cook a steak" and it will do the rest. Due to this machines' integration, you can spend a minimum of 6 minutes in your kitchen doing prep work while cooking steak and a side of veggies.

This device is quite powerful – 1100 watts of power, so it heats up your water pretty quick. The maximum capacity of water as per the manufacturer's recommendation when cooking with a cover is 5 gallons and 2.5 gallons without the cover. This is enough to accommodate a small dinner party or a large family. Considering its power and speed, it is surprisingly quiet sounds as loud as boiling water.

Now that you have the right appliances for the cooking, you need to also get the necessary cooking accessories. By this, I mean stuff like packaging materials etc.

Sous Vide Packaging

1: Zip lock style bags

What are they: They are the easiest way to begin sous vide but you will need a sturdy high-quality product. They are easy to find and affordable. The gallon- sized bags are big enough to contain several servings of food per bag

Where to find them: Remember to choose high quality bags. *When to use:* When cooking all sorts of food, you want to sous vide burgers, chicken breasts, pork chops, fish and pork.

When not to use: The zip-lock bags can fail at temperatures above 158 degrees F (70 degrees C) thereby exposing your food to the water bath. At such temperature, opt for heavy duty sous vide bags.

2: Plastic wrap

What is it? It's the material you use to cover a Tupperware container when you lose the lid.

Where to find it: Buy high quality wrap on at your supermarket buy on bulk, off-brand. Sketchy wrap may not be safe for sous vide.

When to use: It is used to contain and shape foods that need to set such as Hi-Tech mushroom and veggie burgers. When the preparation requires longer cooking times, the plastic covered cylinder is wrapped in a vacuum sealed pouch in order to ensure the packaging does not fail this is not necessary for shorter cooking times.

You can also use it cover the water bath to reduce evaporation especially for the longer cooking times.

When not to use: Generally, sous vide bags and zip-lock bags are the better option when cooking sous vide. Plastic wrap is not suggested as a substitute unless it is specifically recommended.

3: Sous vide bags

What are they: They are sacks with strong seams specifically designed for higher temperature (above 158 degrees F/70 degree C). They are vacuum sealable but don't require a vacuum sealer to work —you simply drape bag's opening over the side of the pot and secure it there or clip it with the lid.

Where to find them:

When to use: they are the best option when cooking foods that need temperatures above 158 degrees F/ 70 degrees C – certain braised meats, beans, lentils and vegetables. They are good for any sous vide preparation. You will find them more helpful especially if you have a vacuum sealer, as they help in keeping food fresher for longer.

4: Canning jars

What are they? They are materials used for pickling and canning; therefore, they are quite easy to come by and are perfect for you if you prefer to avoid plastics.

Where to find them: Thrift shops, grocery store etc.

When to use: When batch cooking something

that needs to set such as yogurt, pates and custard.

When not to use: Don't use canning jars when time is limited. Food takes longer to cook when using canning jars so, use plastic bags when you are short on time.

With all we've learned in mind, let's briefly discuss some tips and tricks guaranteed to make your sous vide cooking a great success.

Chapter 2: Tips and Tricks for Success in Sous Vide Cooking

1: Add ping pong balls to your water bath

If you sous vide for a long time, the water bath can dip to such a low level that the circulator will completely shut off. This disrupts your cooking time and can be a serious risk of food safety. You could choose to cover the water bath with aluminum foil or plastic wrap to prevent evaporation or curve out a hole shaped like a sous vide device from an appropriate fitting lid but the easiest solution is to add a layer of ping-pong balls into the water bath.

The layer of ping-pong balls on the surface of the water bath simultaneously helps the steam to condense and drip back to the bath and insulates the water bath. The ping-pong balls conform to whatever shape of the container you are using and allows you to drop the vacuum sealed bags in and fish them out of the bath mid cook. The ping-pong balls are also reusable.

2: Submerge the sous vide bags with a binder clip

Floating bags is a common sous vide difficulty.

There are a few reasons for this such as an imperfect seal where the air is trapped in the bag to begin with. (this is most common when using water displacement method). With prolonged cooks or high temperatures, vapor can also be formed inside the bag as the water gets heated and evaporates, or as air bubbles, which are trapped inside the veggies or meat escape. The sous vide bags can also float when cooking food that is less dense than water. It is quite vital for the bags to remain submerged and the trapped air bubbles to be pushed to the top away from the food while sous vide cooking. This is to guarantee that the food gets heat properly, which is important for both the food quality and safety.

So, how do you get the floating bags to sink? All you need to do is to use a big binder clip to clamp the bottom of your bag after which you put a pretty heavy spoon in the mouth of the clip. The spoons head keeps it from falling out and the weight of the spoon keeps the bags of the food submerged. You can add a few spoons to especially stubborn bags.

3: Use water displacement to seal zipper top bags
No vacuum sealer? No worry. Vacuum sealers are designed to remove air from plastic bags while sous vide cooking but they are prohibitively expensive. The good news is that there is an easier, quicker and cheaper option referred to as the water displacement method. It only requires a pot or tub of water and a zipper lock freezer bag.

To do water displacement, begin by placing food inside the zip lock bag then seal the bag leaving open the last inch of the seal. Next, lower the bag into a tub or a pot of water. As you lower the bag into the water, the water pressure pushes air out of the bag via the small opening you left. Seal off the opening just before the bag is completely submerged and pull out the whole bag from the tub.

Before we get to the recipes, let's have a comprehensive discussion on how sous vide works.

How Sous Vide Works

You begin by placing the food you want to cook in a vacuum seal bag then remove air from inside the bag using a vacuum sealer or water displacement method. The vacuum sealer has a fan quite similar to that in a vacuum cleaner, which pulls air from the bag and prevents more air from entering it. The plastic of the sealing bag typically conforms to the shape of the food sealed inside it. Afterwards, you need to seal the air from the vacuum sealer to prevent more air from getting in. This is achieved by using a heated sealing surface, which presses the bag shut and applies some heat to the bag to melt the plastic slightly, which creates a secure airtight seal which can't be pulled apart simply.

Now that the foods are sealed, you heat the water bath next. This process requires a device that allows a stable temp of water, so the more even the heat is and the greater the volume, the better. Ideally, slow cookers and rice cookers such as the Admiral craft RC-E50 are used in this process. We'll use 72-hour short ribs as a good example of sous vide cooking. When you cook meat at a low temperature, it turns the connective tissue into tender mouthwatering deliciousness reason being that firm collagen proteins of the meat begin to denature and change into softer gelatin. When you cook the meat at high temp, it causes the muscle fibers of your meat to toughen.

Since browning of steak is caused by high heat when the short ribs are done cooking, you will have a pale and soft piece of meat because as mentioned earlier, sous vide involves low temp. The browning is usually done after sous vide. The meat would cook for 72 hours at 55 degrees C after which you get your skillet as hot as you can then remove your cooked meat from the water bath. Open your vacuum sealed bag, oil the skillet then adds the meat immediately. Turn the steak with tongs until it is nicely browned on each side and voila, you have perfectly cooked steak.

Cooking Sous Vide Safety

As with all new concepts, people have certain doubts about Sous Vide cooking. Some like to think it is not okay to cook food in plastic bags, while others are concerned about low cooking temperatures. Cooking in plastic this sounds like a wrong decision, and there are some alarming reports. We get your concern, as most of Sous Vide bags are made polyethylene. But there are some other things to have in mind. What about clean kitchen surfaces, and clean equipment? We should put all blame on the plastic bags. And what about plastic food containers, aren't they bad?

Plastic is not okay, but if you buy plastic bags from certified retailers, you can make your food perfectly safe. In the end, plastic is not safe when used over and over again, or at high temperatures. Sous Vide bags should be used only once, and since this appliance does not cook at high temperatures, you will be perfectly okay. We know we love quality, juice, and well-done meat, seafood, and veggies, and why to avoid this, just because we are afraid. Still, if you have doubts, you can use canning jars instead. Another concern when it comes to Sous Vide is bacteria, especially salmonella. Salmonella only thrives in a particular range of temperatures, from 40-

135F. This danger zone is the reason why we keep our food in the refrigerator for an hour before we cook them, or cook food to a particular temperature before we serve and eat them.

There is no need to worry about bacteria, as long you keep your food clean, your kitchen counter clean, and refrigerate before cooking. Once you vacuum-seal you fresh steak or fish and cook it for longer periods of time at a steady temperature, there are no worries that any bacteria will grow. The precision temperature control of Sous Vide means that this method is safe than other traditional methods. Sous Vide is an entirely safe way to cook food, and plastic bags are okay because you are not exposing them to high temperatures. As you see, there is no reason why not to enjoy perfectly cooked and juicy food from the Sous Vide appliance.

Some advantages of using Sous Vide

Some of the core advantages of using Sous Vide are as follows:

- You will be able to capture the beautiful
  "essence" of gourmet flavors

in   your meal without being a master of the trade.

- Since you are not required to stare at the water
bath, it saves a lot of time from your daily life.
- All   of   the   natural   juices   and nutrients   are
perfectly stored in your sealed bags.

- The accurate cooking will allow you to cook all of your expensive cuts of meat to perfect every single time.

Health benefits of Sous Vide

The above-mentioned advantages are not the only good things that are going to come out from your Sous Vide experience, as there are a number of health benefits that you should be aware of as well.

- Sous Vide doesn't require you to add any additional fats or oil while cooking, which helps to make the prepared meal healthier. This allows your body to eventually lower down its cholesterol levels in the long run.
- Meals cooked by Souse Vide method are easier to digest as it helps to break down the collagen proteins into gelatin, which is easier for the body to adapt and absorb.
- Exposing ingredients to heat, oxygen, and water causes them to lose a lot of useful nutrients, which leads to over-carbonization of meats

and vitamin/antioxidant loss in vegetables. Sous Vide requires you to seal your ingredients in a vacuum-sealed pouch, as they don't come in contact with air or water, allowing them to preserve their nutrients.

Sous Vide Cooking Time and Temperature Guidelines

Beef

Steak

Rare
Temperature: 54 degrees C/129 degrees F Time: min 1 hour, max 2 hours

Medium
Temperature: 136 degrees F/58 degrees C Time: min 1 hour, max 2 hours

Well done
Temperature: 154 degrees F/ 68 degrees C Time: min 1 hour, max 2 hours

Roast

Rare
Temperature: 133 degrees F, 36 degrees C Time: min 7 hours, max 16 hours

Medium rare
Temperature: 140 degrees F, 60 degrees C Time: min 6 hours, max 14 hours

Well done
Temperature: 158 degrees F, 70 degrees C Time: min 5

hours, max 11 hours

Tough cuts

Rare

Temperature: 131 degrees
F, 55 degrees C Time: min
24 hours, max 48 hours

Medium rare

Temperature: 149 degrees F,
65 degrees C Time: 24 hours

Well done

Temperature: 185 degrees F,
85 degrees C Time: min 8
hours, max 16 hours

Pork

Chops
Rare
Temperature: 136 degrees F,
58 degrees C Time: min 1
hour, max 3 hours
Medium rare
Temperature: 144 degrees F,
62 degrees C Time: min 1
hour, max 3 hours
Well done
Temperature: 158 degrees F,
70 degrees C Time: min 1
hour, max 3 hours
Roast
Rare
Temperature: 136 degrees
F, 58 degrees C Time: min
3 hours, max 5 ½ hours
Medium rare
Temperature: 144 degrees F,
62 degrees C Time: min 3
hours, max 4 hours
Well done

Temperature: 158 degrees F, 70 degrees C Time: min 3 hours, max 3 ½ hours

Tough cuts

Rare

Temperature: 140 degrees F, 60 degrees C Time: min 8 hours, max 24 hours

Medium rare

Temperature: 154 degrees F, 68 degrees C Time: min 8 hours, max 24 hours

Well done:

Temperature: 185 degrees F,
85 degrees C Time: min 8
hours, max 16 hours

Chicken

Light meat
Super supple
Temperature: 140 degrees F,
60 degrees C Time: min 1
hour, max 3 hours
Tender and juicy
Temperature: 149 degrees F,
65 degrees C Time: min 1
hour, max 3 hours
Well done
Temperature: 167 degrees F,
75 degrees C Time: min 1
hour, max 3 hours
Dark meat
Tender
Temperature: 149 degrees
F, 65 degrees C Time: min
45 minutes, max 5 hours
Falling off the bone
Temperature: 167 degrees F,
75 degrees C Time: min 45
minutes, max 5 hours

Fish

Tender

Temperature: 104 degrees F, 40
degrees C Time: min 40
minutes, max 1 hour 10 minutes

Tender and flaky

Temperature: 122 degrees F, 50
degrees C Time: min 40
minutes, max 1 hour 10 minutes

Well done

Temperature: 131 degrees F, 55 degrees C

Time: min 40 minutes, max 1 hour 10 minutes

Vegetables

Green vegetables
Temperature: 180 degrees F,
82 degrees C Time: min 10
minutes, max 20 minutes
Winter squash
Temperature: 185 degrees F,
85 degrees C Time: min 1
hour, max 3 hours
Potatoes and root vegetables
Temperature: 185 degrees F,
85 degrees C Time: min 2
hours, max 3 hours

Fruit

Warm and ripe
Temperature: 154 degrees F, 68 degrees C
Time: min 1 hour 45 minutes, max 2 hours 30
minutes
*Cooked to soft (for purees and
such)* Temperature: 185 degrees
F, 85 degrees C Time: min 30
minutes, max 1 hour 30 minutes

Now that you know how to cook sous vide, it

is now time we start preparing delicious recipes to get you started with this new way of cooking. In this book, we will discuss delicious sous vide breakfast, lunch, dinner, dessert, snack and drink recipes guaranteed to yield the quality food you deserve:

Chapter 3: Appetizers

Spicy Bacon

Time to prepare: 10 min
Time to cook: 9 h 10 min
Servings: 4

You will need:

- 1 pound bacon, sliced
- 1/2 tsp ground paprika
- 1/2 tsp chili pepper
- Salt and

pepper to taste

Directions:

1. Preheat your cooking machine to 145 degrees F.
2. Mix the ingredients thoroughly but carefully, making sure the bacon slices are evenly covered with spices.
3. Place the ingredients in the vacuum bag.
4. Seal it, set the timer for 9 hours.
5. Preheat the skillet and roast each slice on both sides for 10-15 seconds.
6. Serve hot.

Nutrition per serving: Calories: 360
Protein: 12 g

Fats: 35 g
Carbs: 9 g

Broccoli in Oyster Sauce

Time to prepare: 10 min
Time to cook: 35 min
Servings: 4

You will need:
- 2 cups broccoli florets
- 1 tbsp oyster sauce
- 2 tbsp olive oil
- Salt and pepper to taste
- 1 garlic
clove, minced

Directions:
1. Preheat your cooking machine to 183 degrees F.
2. Mix the ingredients and place them in the vacuum bag.
3. Seal the bag and put it in the water bath, setting the timer for 35 minutes.
4. Carefully mix with the minced garlic clove before serving.

Nutrition per serving: Calories: 160
Protein: 3 g
Fats: 14 g
Carbs: 9 g

Button Mushrooms & Parmesan

Time to prepare: 10 min
Time to cook: 45 min
Servings: 4

You will need:

- 1 pound button mushrooms, coarsely chopped
- 4 tbsp olive oil
- 1 garlic clove, minced
- 1 cup Parmesan cheese, shredded
- 1/4 cup dry white wine
- 2 tbsp black truffle oil
- Salt and

pepper to taste

Directions:

1. Set your cooking device to 180 degrees F.
2. Mix the mushrooms with olive oil, sprinkle with salt and pepper and place them in the vacuum bag. Seal the bag removing the air.
3. Set the timer for 35 minutes.
4. Heat a skillet, add the cooked and drained mushrooms and pour over the white wine.
5. Simmer until the liquid evaporates.
6. Serve sprinkled with the truffle oil and topped with grated

Parmesan cheese.

Nutrition per serving: Calories: 280
Protein: 10 g
Fats: 25 g
Carbs: 7 g

Brussel Sprouts Teriyaki

Time to prepare: 10 min
Time to cook: 35 min
Servings: 4

You will need:

- 1 pound Brussel sprouts
- 2 tbsp Teriyaki sauce
- 2 tbsp olive oil
- Salt and pepper to taste
- 1 garlic

clove, minced

Directions:

1. Set your cooking device to 183 degrees F.
2. In a salad bowl, mix the ingredients and place them in the vacuum bag. Seal the bag removing the air.
3. Put the bag into the water bath and set the cooking time for 35 minutes.
4. Carefully mix the sprouts with the minced garlic clove before serving.

Nutrition per serving: Calories: 159
Protein: 3 g
Fats: 13 g
Carbs: 8 g

Omelette with Herbs & Parmesan
Time to prepare: 10 min
Time to cook: 20 min
Servings: 2

You will need:

- 3 eggs
- 1 tbsp melted butter
- 1/2 tbsp tarragon, minced
- 1/2 tbsp rosemary, minced
- 1 tbsp plain yogurt
- Salt and pepper to taste
- 1 tbsp parsley, finely chopped (for serving)
- 1 tbsp grated

Parmesan (for serving)

Directions:

1. Preheat your cooking machine to 165 degrees F.
2. In a large bowl, whisk eggs with the yogurt, then add the herbs and mix again.
3. Pour the ingredients into the vacuum bag, seal it and put in the water bath.
4. Set the timer for 20 minutes.
5. After cooking the eggs for 10 minutes, carefully remove them and press into the shape of

omelette. Cook for 10 more minutes.

6. Remove the omelette from the bag, wait till it cools down, chop into the portions and serve as a starter garnished with the chopped parsley and grated Parmesan.

Nutrition per serving: Calories: 140 Protein: 15 g

Fats: 12 g
Carbs: 1.7 g

Chicken Fajitas

Time to prepare: 10 min
Time to cook: 1 h 10 min
Servings: 4-6

You will need:

- 2 pounds chicken breast, bones and skin removed, sliced
- 2 green peppers, thinly sliced
- Fajita seasoning to taste
- 1 small onion, finely sliced

Directions:

1. Preheat your cooking machine to 146 degrees F.
2. Place 3-4 breast slices in each vacuum bag, add onions, peppers and Fajita seasoning.
3. Seal the bags and set the timer for 1 hour.
4. After cooking the chicken in the Sous Vide machine, brown the slices in a cast iron skillet over medium heat and serve with tortilla shells, grated Cheddar cheese, sour cream and guacamole.

Nutrition per serving: Calories: 357
Protein: 24 g
Fats: 12 g
Carbs: 40 g

Parmesan & Turkey Bites with Pesto

Time to prepare: 10 min
Time to cook: 1 h 10 min
Servings: 4-6

You will need:

- 2 pounds turkey breast, bones and skin removed, sliced
- 1 small onion, finely sliced
- Sal and pepper to taste
- Parmesan cheese, grated
- Pesto sauce

Directions:

1. Preheat your cooking machine to 146 degrees F.
2. Place 3-4 breast slices in each vacuum bag, add onions, season with salt and pepper.
3. Seal the bags and set the timer for 1 hour.
4. After cooking the turkey in the Sous Vide machine, brown the slices in a cast iron skillet over medium heat from one side.
5. Then turn the slices to the other side, sprinkle each with grated parmesan and let the cheese melt.
6. Serve as an appetizer with Pesto sauce.

Nutrition per serving:
Calories: 160
Protein: 15 g
Fats: 10 g
Carbs: 5 g

Salmon & Avocado Bites

Time to prepare: 10 min
Time to cook: 1 h
Servings: 4-6

You will need:

- 1 salmon fillet
- Salt and pepper to taste
- 12 baguette crostini
- 1 ripe avocado
- Lemon juice for sprinkling
  Directions:
  1. Preheat your cooking machine to 104 degrees F.
  2. Sprinkle salmon fillet with salt and place it into the vacuum bag.
  3. Seal it, setting the timer for 1 hour.
  4. When the fillet is cooked, let it cool down, slice with a sharp knife and serve over baguette crostini topped with mashed avocado and sprinkled with lemon juice.

Nutrition per serving:
Calories: 120
Protein: 8 g
Fats: 3 g
Carbs: 15 g

Salmon & Tartar Toasts

Time to prepare: 10 min
Time to cook: 1 h
Servings: 4-6

You will need:

- 1 salmon fillet
- Salt and pepper to taste
- 10-12 toasts
- 1/2 cup sour cream
- 1 marinated cucumber
- 4

dill
sprigs
Directio
ns:

1. Preheat your cooking machine to 104 degrees F.
2. Sprinkle salmon fillet with salt and place it into the vacuum bag.
3. Seal it, setting the timer for 1 hour.
4. While the fillet is cooking, make the tartar sauce. To do this, mix the sour cream with finely chopped marinated cucumber and freshly chopped dill.
5. When the fillet is cooked, let it cool down, slice with a sharp knife and serve over toasts,

topped with the tartar sauce.

Nutrition per serving: Calories: 120
Protein: 8 g
Fats: 3 g
Carbs: 15 g

Poached Eggs Toast

Time to prepare: 10 min
Time to cook: 15 min
Servings: 4

You will need:

- 4 eggs
- 4 bread toasts
- 1 avocado, mashed
- Salt and pepper to taste

Directions:

1. Preheat your cooking machine to 167 degrees F.
2. Carefully merge the eggs into the water, making sure you don't crack them.
3. Set the cooking time for 15 minutes.
4. When the time is up, run the eggs under cold water for 5-10 second and then remove the shell.
5. Serve over toasts, spread with mashed avocado and sprinkled with salt and pepper.

Nutrition per serving:
Calories: 298
Protein: 11 g
Fats: 19 g
Carbs: 24 g

Beef Meatballs

Preparation time: 10 minutes
Cooking time: 3 hours
Servings: 12

Ingredients:

- 1 pound beef, ground
- 2 tablespoons milk
- Salt and black pepper to the taste
- 1 egg
- 1 tablespoon flour
- ½ shallot, chopped
- 2 tablespoons parsley, chopped
- 1 tablespoon oregano, dried
- 1 tablespoon garlic powder
- 3 tablespoons parmesan, grated

Directions:

1. In a bowl, mix the beef with milk, salt, pepper, egg, flour, shallot, parsley, oregano, garlic and parmesan, stir well and shape medium meatballs out of this mix.

2. Put all the meatballs in a sous vide bag, seal it and freeze them for 1 hour.

3. Submerge the bag into the preheated water bath, cook them at 140 degrees F for 1 hour, arrange them on a platter and serve as an appetizer.

Enjoy!

Nutrition: calories 220, fat 6, carbs 14, protein 7

French Style Escargots

Preparation time: 10 minutes
Cooking time: 6 hours and 5 minutes
Servings: 4
Ingredients:

- 24 French snails, cleaned and intestines removed
- 2 carrots, chopped
- 1 and ½ cup chicken stock
- 1 bay leaf
- 1 yellow onion, chopped
- Salt and black pepper to the taste
- 3 rosemary springs, chopped

For serving:

- 2 tablespoons butter, melted
- 1 tablespoon shallot, chopped
- 1 tablespoon garlic, minced
- ¼ cup chicken stock
- 2 tablespoons cilantro, chopped

Directions:

1. In a big sous vide bag, combine the snails with carrots, 1 and ½ cup stock, bay leaf, onion, salt, pepper and rosemary, seal the bag, shake it, submerge it in the preheated water oven and cook at 154 degrees F for 6 hours.
2. Heat up a pan with the ghee over medium-high heat, add shallot, garlic and ¼ cup stock, sauté for 4-5 minutes, also add drained snails,

toss, cook for 1-2 minutes more, arrange them all on a platter, sprinkle the cilantro on top and serve. Enjoy!

Nutrition: calories 231, fat 3, carbs 15, protein 6

Cheese Spread

Preparation time: 10 minutes
Cooking time: 30 minutes
Servings: 4

Ingredients:

- 2 cups Mexican cheese, shredded
- ¼ cup heavy cream
- 4 ounces canned green chilies, drained and chopped
- 2 tablespoons yellow onion, grated
- 2 teaspoons cumin, ground
- A pinch of salt and white pepper

Directions:

1. In a sous vide bag, mix the cheese with the cream, chilies, onion, cumin, salt and pepper, seal the bag, submerge in the preheated water bath, cook at 175 degrees F for 30 minutes, transfer to a bowl, blend using an immersion blender, divide into small bowls and serve as an appetizer.

Enjoy!

Nutrition: calories 160, fat 14, carbs 15, protein 6

Shrimp Wraps

Preparation time: 10 minutes
Cooking time: 33 minutes
Servings: 16

Ingredients:

- 2 tablespoons olive oil
- 16 shrimps, peeled and deveined
- 1 tablespoons mint, chopped
- 1/3 cup blackberries, ground
- 16 prosciutto slices
- 1/3 cup red wine

Directions:

1. Wrap each shrimp in a prosciutto slice, introduce them into sous vide bags, seal, submerge in the preheated water oven and cook at 140 degrees F for 30 minutes.

2. Heat up a pan with the blackberries over medium heat, add mint and the wine, stir, cook for 2 minutes, add the wrapped shrimp, toss gently for 1 minute more, arrange on a platter and serve.

Enjoy!

Nutrition: calories 255, fat 12, carbs 16, protein 8

Delicious Crab Dip

Preparation time: 10 minutes
Cooking time: 30 minutes
Servings: 8

Ingredients:

- 8 bacon strips, cooked and chopped
- 12 ounces crab meat
- ½ cup mayonnaise
- ½ cup heavy cream
- 8 ounces cream cheese, soft
- 2 poblano peppers, chopped
- 2 tablespoons lime juice
- Salt and black pepper to the taste
- 4 garlic cloves, minced
- 4 green onions, minced
- ½ cup parmesan cheese, grated
- Salt and black pepper to the taste

Directions:

1. In a bowl, mix the cream with cream cheese, mayo, parmesan, poblano peppers, bacon, green onion, garlic, salt, pepper and lemon juice and whisk.

2. Put crab meat in a sous vide bag, seal, submerge in the preheated water bath, cook at 154 degrees F for 30 minutes, add to the bowl, whisk and serve.

Enjoy!

Nutrition: calories 210, fat 7, carbs 14, protein 9

Mexican Stuffed Mushrooms

Preparation time: 10 minutes
Cooking time: 1 hour
Servings: 4

Ingredients:

- ¼ cup mayonnaise
- 1 teaspoon garlic powder
- 1 small yellow onion, chopped
- 24 ounces white mushroom caps
- Salt and black pepper to the taste
- 4 ounces cream cheese, soft
- ¼ cup heavy cream
- ½ cup Mexican cheese, shredded
- 1 cup shrimp, cooked, peeled, deveined and chopped

Directions:

1. In a bowl, mix the mayo with garlic powder, onion, curry powder, cream cheese, coconut cream, Mexican cheese, shrimp, salt and pepper, stir, stuff the mushrooms with this mix, put them in a sous vide bag, seal it, submerge in preheated water bath and cook at 180 degrees F for 1 hour.

2. Serve as an appetizer.

Enjoy!

Nutrition: calories 224, fat 12, carbs 16, protein 11

Italian Chicken Wings

Preparation time: 10 minutes
Cooking time: 4 hours and 10 minutes
Servings: 6
Ingredients:
- 6 pounds chicken wings, halved
- Salt and black pepper to the taste
- ½ teaspoon Italian seasoning
- 2 tablespoons olive oil
- ½ cup parmesan cheese, grated
- 1 teaspoon garlic powder
- 1 egg

Directions:
1. Season the chicken wings with salt and pepper, add half of the oil, put them in a sous vide bag, seal, submerge them in preheated water bath and cook at 170 degrees F for 4 hours.
2. Meanwhile, in your blender, mix the rest of the oil with the cheese, egg, garlic powder and Italian seasoning and blend
3. Transfer chicken wings to baking sheet, add the mix from the blender, toss, broil them for 5 minutes, arrange on a platter and serve. Enjoy!

Nutrition: calories 254, fat 8, carbs 20, protein 17

Cheesy Artichoke Dip

Preparation time: 10 minutes
Cooking time: 1 hour and 10 minutes
Servings: 12

Ingredients:

- 1 cup heavy cream
- ¼ cup mayonnaise
- ¼ cup spring onions, chopped
- 1 tablespoon olive oil
- 2 garlic cloves, minced
- 4 ounces cream cheese, soft
- 1 cup mozzarella cheese, shredded
- 4 ounces feta cheese, crumbled
- 1 tablespoon balsamic vinegar
- 28 ounces artichoke hearts
- Salt and black pepper to the taste
- 10 ounces spinach, chopped

Directions:

1. In a sous vide bag, mix the artichokes with salt, pepper and spinach, seal the bag, submerge in the preheated water bath, cook at 183 degrees F for 1 hour, chop and put them in a bowl.

2. Heat up a pan with the oil over medium heat, add onions and garlic and sauté for 3-4 minutes.

3. Add cream, cream cheese, mayo, feta cheese, mozzarella, the artichokes, spinach,

salt, pepper and the vinegar, stir, cook for 5 minutes more, divide into bowls and serve. Enjoy!

Nutrition: calories 264, fat 12, carbs 17, protein 8

Simple Oysters

Preparation time: 10 minutes
Cooking time: 30 minutes
Servings: 3

Ingredients:

- 6 oysters, shucked
- 3 garlic cloves, minced
- 1 lemon, cut into wedges
- 1 tablespoon parsley, chopped
- 1 teaspoon smoked paprika
- 2 tablespoons butter, melted

Directions:

1. Stuff the oysters with the butter, parsley and paprika, put them in separate sous vide bags, seal, submerge them in the preheated water oven, cook them at 120 degrees F for 30 minutes, arrange on a platter and serve with lemon wedges on the side.

Enjoy!

Nutrition: calories 215, fat 1, carbs 20, protein 8

Parmesan Salmon Bites

Preparation time: 10 minutes
Cooking time: 40 minutes
Servings: 4
Ingredients:
- 4 garlic cloves, minced
- 2 pounds salmon fillets, skinless, boneless and cubed
- Salt and black pepper to the taste
- ½ cup parmesan, grated
- ¼ cup cilantro, chopped

Directions:
1. Put the salmon bites in a sous vide bag, add salt and pepper, seal the bag, submerge it in the preheated water bath, cook them at 130 degrees F for 40 minutes and spread on a lined baking sheet.
2. Sprinkle cilantro, garlic and parmesan, broil over medium heat for 5 minutes and serve as an appetizer.

Enjoy!

Nutrition: calories 240, fat 12, carbs 20, protein 17

Chapter 4: Vegetables

Cream of Corn Soup

Time to prepare: 10 min
Time to cook: 40 min
Servings: 4

You will need:
- Kernels of 4 corn ears
- 6 cups still water
- 1 cup heavy cream
- 1 tbsp olive oil
- Salt and

pepper to taste

Directions:
1. Set your cooking device to 183 degrees F.
2. Place the kernels, salt, pepper and olive oil into the plastic bag, and seal it, removing the air.
3. Set the cooking time for 25 minutes.
4. Transfer the cooked kernels with the liquid to a pot. Add the cream and still water (if needed) and simmer on a medium heat for about 10 minutes.
5. Blend the soup with an immersion

blender, and salt and pepper if
needed and serve with chopped
parsley.

Nutrition per serving: Calories: 105
Protein: 4 g
Fats: 3 g
Carbs: 18 g

Cold Pea & Yogurt Soup

Time to prepare: 10 min
Time to cook: 1 h
Servings: 4

You will need:

- 1 onion, chopped
- 2 garlic cloves, minced
- 1 carrot, peeled and grated
- 1 1/2 cups frozen peas
- 2 cups vegetable stock
- Salt and pepper to taste
- Greek yogurt for serving
- Chopped dill or

cilantro for serving Directions:

1. Set your cooking device to 183 degrees F.
2. Place the onion, garlic and carrot into the vacuum bag, and seal it, removing the air.
3. Set the cooking time for 50 minutes.
4. Blend the cooked vegetable with the stock using an immersion blender, and salt and pepper to taste.
5. Serve refrigerated with yogurt and chopped dill or cilantro.

Nutrition per serving: Calories: 135
Protein: 7 g
Fats: 1 g
Carbs: 27 g

Potato & Curry Soup

Time to prepare: 10 min
Time to cook: 1 h
Servings: 4

You will need:

- 1 onion, chopped
- 2 garlic cloves, minced
- 1 carrot, peeled and grated
- 1 1/2 cup potato, peeled and cubed
- 2 cups vegetable stock
- Salt and pepper to taste
- 2 tbsp curry powder
- Chopped

cilantro for serving

Directions:

1. Preheat the cooking device to 183 degrees F.
2. Put the vegetables and curry powder into the vacuum bag, and seal it, removing the air.
3. Set the cooking time for 50 minutes.
4. Transfer the cooked vegetables to a pot, add the vegetable stock and blend everything together using an immersion blender.
5. Bring the soup to boil and simmer for 2-3 minutes.
6. Add salt and pepper to taste.

7. Serve with yogurt and chopped dill or cilantro.

Nutrition per serving:
Calories: 355
Protein: 11 g
Fats: 17 g
Carbs: 42 g

Carrot & Celery Soup

Time to prepare: 10 min
Time to cook: 2 h 30 min
Servings: 4

You will need:

- 2 medium carrots, peeled and chopped
- 1 celery stalk, chopped
- 1 yellow onion, peeled and chopped
- 2 garlic cloves, minced
- 1 tsp dried rosemary
- 2 bay leaves
- 6 cups vegetable stock
- Salt and

pepper to taste

Directions:

1. Preheat the cooking device to 183 degrees F.
2. Put the ingredients into the vacuum bag, and seal it, removing the air.
3. Set the cooking time for 2 hours 10 minutes.
4. Transfer the cooked vegetables with the liquid into a pot.
5. Add the vegetable stock, bring to boil and simmer for 10 more minutes.
6. Blend everything together using an immersion blender.

7. Serve with yogurt and chopped dill or cilantro.

Nutrition per serving:
Calories: 80
Protein: 5 g
Fats: 1g
Carbs: 16 g

Butter Potatoes

Time to prepare: 10 min
Time to cook: 1 h
Servings: 4

You will need:
- 1 pounds potatoes, peeled
- 4 tsp unsalted butter
- 1 tsp olive oil
- 4 tbsp chopped parsley
- Salt and

pepper to taste

Directions:
1. Preheat your Sous Vide machine to 190 degrees F
2. Put the potatoes into the vacuum bag, add butter and olive oil. Season with salt and pepper.
3. Seal the bag, put it into the water bath and set the timer for 1 hour.
4. Serve immediately with

chopped parsley.

Nutrition per serving:
Calories: 160
Protein: 4 g
Fats: 9 g
Carbs: 22 g

Garlic Brussels Sprouts

Time to prepare: 10 min
Time to cook: 1 h
Servings: 4

You will need:

- 1 pound fresh Brussels sprouts
- 2 garlic cloves, minced
- 1 tbsp olive oil
- Salt and

pepper to taste

Directions:

1. Preheat your Sous Vide machine to 180 degrees F
2. Put the sprouts into the vacuum bag, add the olive oil, garlic salt and pepper to taste.
3. Seal the bag, put it into the water bath and set the timer for 1 hour.
4. When the time is up, serve with any preferred sauce.

Nutrition per serving: Calories: 43
Protein: 2 g
Fats: 2.2 g
Carbs: 5.5 g

Mixed Vegetables with Butter

Time to prepare: 10 min
Time to cook: 3 h 10 min
Servings: 4

You will need:
- 2 big carrots, peeled and chopped
- 1 turnip, peeled and chopped
- 1 parsnip, peeled and chopped
- 1 medium onion, peeled and sliced
- 2 garlic cloves, minced
- 2 tbsp olive oil
- 1 tbsp dried rosemary
- 2 tbsp unsalted butter
- Salt and

pepper to taste

Directions:
1. Preheat your Sous Vide machine to 185 degrees F
2. In a big bowl, mix all the chopped vegetables.
3. Divide the vegetables into equal parts and put them into vacuum bags, add the olive oil, salt and pepper to taste.
4. Put it into the water bath and set the timer for 3 hours.
5. When the time is up, brown the cooked vegetables in a cast iron

skillet on the high heat with 2 tbsp unsalted butter just until golden.

6. Add freshly minced garlic clove and dried rosemary, mix well with a spoon and close the skillet with a lid for a couple of minutes.

7. Serve as a side dish or a separate vegetarian meal.

Nutrition per serving:

Calories: 219
Protein: 6 g
Fats: 12 g
Carbs: 21 g

Mashed Potatoes

Time to prepare: 10 min
Time to cook: 1 h 40 min
Servings: 4

You will need:

- 1 pounds potatoes, peeled and sliced
- 4 garlic cloves, minced
- 2 rosemary sprigs
- 1 cup milk
- 1 tsp salt

Directions:

1. Preheat your Sous Vide machine to 194 degrees F
2. Put the sliced potatoes into the vacuum bag, add other ingredients.
3. Seal the bag, put it into the water bath and set the timer for 1 hour 30 min.
4. When the time is up, remove the rosemary sprigs, and mash the potatoes with the liquid in a big bowl.

Serve immediately. Nutrition per serving: Calories: 160
Protein: 4 g
Fats: 9 g
Carbs: 22 g

Cabbage Wedges

Time to prepare: 10 min
Time to cook: 4 h
Servings: 6

You will need:

- 1 small cabbage head, cut into 6 wedges
- 2-4 tsp butter
- 1 tsp salt

  Directions:

  1. Preheat your Sous Vide machine to 190 degrees F
  2. Put the sliced cabbage into the vacuum bags, adding 1 tsp butter to each bag.
  3. Seal the bag, put it into the water bath and set the timer for 4 hours.
  4. When the time is up, brown the wedges in 1 tsp butter in a cast iron skillet until golden on both sides.
  5. Serve immediately

with sour cream. Nutrition per serving:

Calories: 107

Protein: 3 g

Fats: 9 g

Carbs: 11 g

Assorted Mushrooms with Herbs and Sour Cream

Time to prepare: 10 min
Time to cook: 30 min
Servings: 4

You will need:

- 1 pound assorted mushrooms, washed and chopped
- 2 tbsp sugar-free soy sauce
- Salt and pepper to taste
- 1 tbsp olive oil
- 2 tbsp freshly chopped parsley for serving
- 2 tbsp sour cream for serving

Directions:

1. Preheat your Sous Vide machine to 180 degrees F
2. Place all ingredients in the vacuum bag.
3. Seal the bag, put it into the water bath and set the timer for 30 minutes.
4. When the time is up, serve immediately with sour cream and chopped parsley.

Nutrition per serving: Calories: 58
Protein: 3 g

Fats: 6 g
Carbs: 2 g

Asparagus

Time to prepare: 10 min
Time to cook: 1 h
Servings: 4

You will need:

- 1 pound asparagus
- 1 garlic clove, minced
- 1 tbsp olive oil
- Juice of 1/2 lemon
- Salt and

pepper to taste

Directions:

1. Preheat your Sous Vide machine to 135 degrees F
2. Place all ingredients in the vacuum bag.
3. Seal the bag, put it into the water bath and set the timer for 1 hour.
4. When the time is up, serve immediately as a side dish or a starter.

Nutrition per serving: Calories: 27
Protein: 4.4 g
Fats: 2 g
Carbs: 3 g

Butter Carrots

Time to prepare: 10 min
Time to cook: 1 h
Servings: 4

You will need:

- 1 pound small carrots, peeled
- 2 tbsp butter
- Salt and pepper to taste
- 1 tbsp brown sugar Directions:
  1. Preheat your Sous Vide machine to 185 degrees F
  2. Place all ingredients in the vacuum bag.
  3. Seal the bag, put it into the water bath and set the timer for 1 hour.
  4. When the time is up, serve immediately as a side dish or a starter.

Nutrition
per
serving:
Calories:
100
Protein: 1 g
Fats: 4 g
Carbs: 15 g

Asian Style Eggplants

Time to prepare: 10 min
Time to cook: 1 h
Servings: 4

You will need:

- 1 pound eggplants, sliced
- 2 tbsp sugar-free soy sauce
- 6 tbsp sesame oil
- 1 tbsp sesame seeds for serving
- Salt and pepper to taste

Directions:

1. Preheat your Sous Vide machine to 185 degrees F
2. Place all ingredients in the vacuum bag.
3. Seal the bag, put it into the water bath and set the timer for 50 min.
4. When the time is up, brown the eggplants in cast iron skillet for a couple of minutes.
5. Serve immediately sprinkled with sesame seeds.

Nutrition per serving:
Calories: 78
Protein: 3 g
Fats: 3 g
Carbs: 1 g

Butter Corn on the Cob

Time to prepare: 10 min
Time to cook: 30 min
Servings: 4

You will need:

- 4 corn ears, washed and trimmed
- 2 tbsp butter
- Salt to taste
- 2-3

parsley sprigs

Directions:

1. Preheat your Sous Vide machine to 185 degrees F
2. Place the corn ears into the vacuum bag, add butter, salt and parsley.
3. Seal the bag, put it into the water bath and set the timer for 30 min.
4. When the time is up, remove parsley sprigs and serve the corn.

Nutrition per serving: Calories: 77
Protein: 2 g
Fats: 12 g
Carbs: 16 g

Spicy Chinese Style Green Beans

Time to prepare: 10 min
Time to cook: 1 h
Servings: 4

You will need:

- 1 pound long green beans
- 2 tbsp chili sauce
- 2 garlic cloves, minced
- 1 tbsp onion powder
- 1 tbsp sesame oil
- Salt to taste
- 2 tbsp sesame

seeds for serving Directions:

1. Preheat your Sous Vide machine to 185 degrees F.
2. Place the ingredients in the vacuum bag.
3. Seal the bag, put it into the water bath and set the timer for 1 hour.
4. Sprinkle the beans with sesame

seeds and serve.

Nutrition per serving:
Calories: 62
Protein: 2 g
Fats: 3 g
Carbs: 8 g

Chapter 5: Fruits

Rosemary Apricots

Time to prepare: 10 min
Time to cook: 20 min
Servings: 6

You will need:

- 6 ripe apricots, halved and stone removed
- 1/5 cup water
- 1/5 cup sugar
- 2

rosemary
sprigs

Directions:

1. Set your cooking device to 158 degrees F.
2. In a small saucepan, combine water and sugar, heat the mixture to dissolve the sugar and make the syrup.
3. Bring the syrup to boil and then cool it down.
4. Carefully pour the syrup into the vacuum bag, add the apricot halves, rosemary sprigs and cook in the preheated water bath for 20 minutes.

5. When the time is up, remove the rosemary sprigs and serve the apricots.

Nutrition per serving: Calories: 50
Protein: 0.1 g
Fats: 0 g
Carbs: 13 g

Vanilla Pears

Time to prepare: 10 min
Time to cook: 20 min
Servings: 6

You will need:

- 3 ripe pears, peeled, halved and cored
- 1/5 cup water
- 1/5 cup sugar
- 1 vanilla pod, seeds removed
- 1 anise star

Directions:

1. Set your cooking device to 185 degrees F.
2. In a small saucepan, combine water and sugar, heat the mixture to dissolve the sugar and make the syrup.
3. Bring the syrup to boil and then cool it down.
4. Carefully pour the syrup into the vacuum bag, add the pear halves, vanilla pod and anise star, and cook in the preheated water bath for 20 minutes.
5. When the time is up, remove the vanilla pod and anise star and serve

the pears.

Nutrition per serving: Calories: 35
Protein: 0 g
Fats: 0 g
Carbs: 9 g

Cinnamon Apples

Time to prepare: 10 min
Time to cook: 20 min
Servings: 6

You will need:

- 3 ripe apples, peeled, halved and cored
- 1/5 cup water
- 1/5 cup sugar
- 1 tsp

ground cinnamon

Directions:

1. Set your cooking device to 185 degrees F.
2. In a small saucepan, combine water and sugar, heat the mixture to dissolve the sugar and make the syrup.
3. Bring the syrup to boil and then cool it down.
4. Carefully pour the syrup into the vacuum bag, add the apple halves and cinnamon, and cook in the preheated water bath for 20 minutes.
5. Serve the apples with ice-cream or vanilla sauce.

Nutrition per serving:
Calories: 50

Protein: 0 g
Fats: 0 g
Carbs: 13 g

Poached Sugar Plums

Time to prepare: 10 min
Time to cook: 20 min
Servings: 4

You will need:

- 8 ripe plums, halved, stone removed
- 1/5 cup sugar
- 1 tsp

ground cinnamon

Directions:

1. Set your cooking device to 158 degrees F.
2. In a small bowl, mix the sugar with the cinnamon.
3. Carefully put the halved plums into the vacuum bag, sprinkle them with the sugar-cinnamon mixture, and cook in the preheated water bath for 20 minutes.
4. Serve the plums with vanilla ice-cream.

Nutrition per serving:
Calories: 35
Protein: 0 g
Fats: 0 g
Carbs: 9 g

Tangerine Ice Cream

Time to prepare: 10 min
Time to cook: 30 min + 24 h
Servings: 6

You will need:

- 1 cup mandarin (only juice and pulp)
- 2 cups heavy cream
- 6 fresh egg yolks
- 1/2 cup milk
- 1/2 cup white sugar
- 1/4 cup sweet condensed milk
- A

pinch of
salt

Directions:

1. In a big bowl, combine all ingredients and whisk well until even.
2. Carefully pour the mixture into the vacuum bag and seal it.
3. Cook for 30 minutes in the water bath, previously preheated to 185 degrees F.
4. When the time is up, quick chill the vacuum bag without opening it. To do this, put it into big bowl or container, filled with ice and

water.

5. Refrigerate the vacuum bag with ice-cream for 24 hours.

6. Carefully transfer the mixture to an ice-cream machine and cook according to the instructions.

Nutrition per serving: Calories: 144
Protein: 3 g
Fats: 8 g
Carbs: 17 g

Citrus Confit

Time to prepare: 10 min
Time to cook: 1 h
Servings: 10-15

You will need:

- 2 lemons, sliced and cut into quarters
- 1 orange, sliced and cut into quarters
- 1 lime, sliced and cut into quarters
- 1/2 cup sugar
- 1

/2 cup
salt

Directio
ns:

1. In a big bowl, combine all ingredients and mix well, making sure that fruits are evenly covered with salt and sugar.
2. Carefully put the mixture into the vacuum bag and seal it.
3. Cook for 1 hour in the water bath, previously preheated to 185 degrees F.
4. This confit is very rich in vitamins and can be stored in the fridge for at least 1 month.

Nutrition per serving: Calories: 90
Protein: 1 g

Fats: 2 g
Carbs: 17 g

Raspberry Compote

Time to prepare: 10 min
Time to cook: 1 h
Servings: 4

You will need:

- 1 cups raspberries
- 1 lemon zest
- 1 orange zest
- 1

tbsp white
sugar

Directions:

1. Put the ingredients into the vacuum bag and seal it.
2. Cook for 1 hour in the water bath, previously preheated to 185 degrees F.
3. Serve over ice

cream or cake. Nutrition
per serving:

Calories: 106 Protein:2 g Fats: 1 g Carbs: 25g

Strawberry Jam

Time to prepare: 10 min
Time to cook: 1 h 30 min
Servings: 10

You will need:

- 2 cups strawberries, coarsely chopped
- 1 cup white sugar
- 2 tbsp orange juice Directions:
    4. Put the ingredients into the vacuum bag and seal it.
    5. Cook for 1 hour 30 min in the water bath, previously preheated to 180 degrees F.
    6. Serve over ice cream or cheese cake, or store in the fridge in an airtight container.

Nutrition per serving: Calories: 50
Protein: 0 g
Fats: 0 g
Carbs: 13 g

Peach and Orange Jam

Time to prepare: 10 min
Time to cook: 2 h
Servings: 10

You will need:

- 2 cups peaches, coarsely chopped
- 1 1/2 cup white sugar
- 1 cup water
- Zest and

juice of 1 orange

Directions:

1. Put the ingredients into the vacuum bag and seal it.
2. Cook for 2 hours in the water bath, previously preheated to 190 degrees F.
3. Serve over ice cream or cake, or store in the fridge in an airtight container.

Nutrition per serving: Calories: 50
Protein: 0 g
Fats: 0 g
Carbs: 14 g

Blueberry Jam

Time to prepare: 10 min
Time to cook: 1 h 30 min
Servings: 10

You will need:

- 2 cups blueberries
- 1 cup white sugar
- 2

tbsp lemon
juice

Directions:

1. Preheat the water bath to 180 degrees F.
2. Put the ingredients into the vacuum bag and seal it.
3. Cook for 1 hour 30 min in the water bath.
4. Serve over ice cream or cake, or store in the fridge in an airtight container.

Nutrition per
serving:
Calories: 50
Protein: 0 g
Fats: 0 g
Carbs: 13 g

Chapter 6: Fish

Salmon Gravlox

Time to prepare: 30 min
Time to cook: 1 h
Servings: 8

You will need:

- 8 salmon fillets
- 4 tbsp sugar
- 4

tbsp
salt
Directi
ons:

1. Preheat your cooking machine to 104 degrees F.
2. In a small bowl, mix the sugar with salt.
3. Season the salmon with the mixture and set aside for half an hour.
4. Rinse the salmon fillets and place them into the vacuum bag.
5. Seal it, setting the timer for 1 hour.
6. Serve immediately with toasted bread and cream cheese.

Nutrition per serving: Calories: 260
Protein: 35 g
Fats: 11 g

Carbs: 7 g

Salmon Teriyaki

Time to prepare: 30 min
Time to cook: 1 h
Servings: 8

You will need:

- 8 salmon fillets
- 8 tbsp

Teriyaki sauce

Directions:

1. Preheat your cooking machine to 104 degrees F.
2. Evenly cover the salmon fillets with the Teriyaki sauce set aside for half an hour.
3. Place the fillets in the vacuum bag.
4. Seal it, setting the timer for 1 hour.
5. Serve immediately with

steamed white rice. Nutrition per serving:

Calories: 277
Protein: 35 g
Fats: 5 g
Carbs: 9 g

Ginger Salmon

Time to prepae: 1 h
Time to cook: 40 min Servings: 2

You will need:

- 2 salmon fillets
- 2 tbsp soy sauce
- 1 tbsp liquid honey
- 1 tbsp sesame oil
- 1 tbsp ginger root, minced
- Chili

pepper to taste

Directions:

1. Put all ingredients into the vacuum bag and set aside for 1 hour to marinate.
2. In the meantime, preheat the water bath to 125 degrees F.
3. Seal the bag and set the timer for 30 minutes.
4. When the time is up, you can serve salmon immediately, or sear it on both sides in a cast iron skillet until it browns a bit and then serve over rice, pouring the juices from the bag over the rice.

Nutrition per serving: Calories: 277
Protein: 35 g
Fats: 5 g
Carbs: 9 g

Salmon in Orange & Butter Sauce

Time to prepare: 10 min
Time to cook: 30 min
Servings: 2

You will need:
For the salmon:

- 2 salmon steaks
- Salt to taste
- 1

tbsp olive
oil For the
butter sauce

- 1 cup water
- 1 shallot, finely chopped
- 1/3 cup freshly squeezed orange juice
- 1 tbsp lemon juice
- A pinch of salt and sugar
- 2

tbsp
butter
Direction
s:

1. Rub the fish with salt and put it
   into the vacuum bag together
   with olive oil.
2. Preheat the water bath to 115 degrees F.
3. Seal the bag and set the timer for 25
   minutes.

4. In the meantime, cook the butter sauce.
5. In a small saucepan, combine water, juices, chopped shallot, salt and pepper. Bring to boil and simmer over medium heat until the amount of liquid is reduced to about 4 tbsp.
6. Mix in the butter, pour over the salmon and serve.

Nutrition per
serving:
Calories: 409

Protein: 45 g Fats: 26g Carbs: 8 g

Oriental Soy & Ginger Fish

Time to prepare: 10 min
Time to cook: 20 min
Servings: 2

You will need:

- 2 medium cod fillets
- 1/3 cup sugarfree soy sauce
- 2 tbsp peanut oil
- 2 tbsp sesame oil
- 2 tbsp ginger root, grated
- 2 garlic

cloves, minced

Directions:

1. In a small pan, saute ginger and garlic in peanut oil until lightly golden.
2. Preheat the water bath to 135 degrees F.
3. Put the fish, the sautéed ginger and garlic and the rest of the ingredients in the vacuum bag.
4. Seal the bag and set the timer

for 20 minutes. Nutrition per serving:

Calories: 361
Protein: 40 g
Fats: 9 g
Carbs: 2 g

Cod in Hollandaise Sauce

Time to prepare: 10 min
Time to cook: 20 min
Servings: 2

You will need:

- 2 medium cod fillets
- 2 tbsp olive oil
- Salt and pepper to taste
- Sous Vide

Hollandaise sauce

Directions:

1. Preheat the water bath to 135 degrees F.
2. Rub the cod fillets with salt and pepper and put the fish and olive oil into the vacuum bag.
3. Seal the bag and set the timer for 20 minutes.
4. Serve with the Sous Vide

Hollandaise sauce. Nutrition per serving:

Calories: 544

Protein: 30 g

Fats: 26 g

Carbs: 40 g

Lemon Cod with Garlic and Capers

Time to prepare: 30 min
Time to cook: 30 min
Servings: 2

You will need:

- 2 medium cod fillets
- 2 tbsp olive oil
- Salt and pepper to taste
- 2 tbsp lemon juice
- 2 tbsp marinated capers
- 4 garlic cloves,

coarsely chopped Directions:

1. Rub the cod fillets with salt, pepper and lemon juice, put the fish into the vacuum bag and set aside for 30 minutes to marinate.
2. Preheat the water bath to 135 degrees F.
3. Add the capers, olive oil and garlic cloves to the vacuum bag.
4. Seal the bag and set the timer

for 30 minutes. Nutrition per serving:

Calories: 170
Protein: 27 g
Fats: 6 g
Carbs: 2 g

Spicy Cobbler

Time to prepare: 30 min
Time to cook: 30 min
Servings: 2

You will need:

- 2 medium cobbler fillets
- 2 tbsp unsalted butter, softened
- 2 garlic cloves, minced
- 1 tsp red chili paste
- 1 tbsp fresh lemon juice
- A pinch of salt

Directions:

1. In a small bowl, combine the softened butter with garlic, chili paste, salt and lemon juice.
2. Rub the cobbler fillets with the butter mixture and set aside.
3. In the meantime, preheat the water bath to 145 degrees F.
4. Seal the bag and set the timer for 30 minutes. Nutrition per serving:

Calories: 544
Protein: 30 g
Fats: 26 g
Carbs: 40 g

Blue Cheese Fish

Time to prepare: 10 min
Time to cook: 20 min
Servings: 2

You will need:

- 2 medium fish fillets of your choice (salmon, cod, trout or other)
- 2 tbsp olive oil
- Salt and pepper to taste
- Sous Vide Blue

Cheese sauce Directions:

1. Preheat the water bath to 135 degrees F.
2. Rub the fish fillets with salt and pepper and put the fish and olive oil into the vacuum bag.
3. Seal the bag and set the timer for 20 minutes.
4. Serve with the Sous Vide Blue

Cheese sauce.

Nutrition per serving:
Calories: 544
Protein: 30 g
Fats: 26 g
Carbs: 40 g

Trout in White Wine

Time to prepare: 10 min
Time to cook: 40 min
Servings: 2

You will need:
For the fish

- 2 medium trout fillets
- 2 tbsp olive oil
- Salt and

pepper to taste For
the sauce

- 1 cup dry white wine
- 1 cup heavy cream
- 1 onion, chopped
- Salt and pepper to taste
- 1

tsp lemon
juice

Directions:

1. Preheat the water bath to 120 degrees F.
2. Rub the trout fillets with salt and pepper and put the fish and olive oil into the vacuum bag.
3. Seal the bag and set the timer for 30 minutes.
4. In the meantime, prepare the wine sauce.
5. Combine the wine, chopped

onion, salt and pepper in a pan
and reduce over medium hit.

6. Mix in the heavy cream.
7. Serve the trout fillets with the
   sauce, sprinkled with lemon
   juice.

Nutrition per serving: Calories: 352
Protein: 35 g
Fats: 22 g
Carbs: 1 g

Trout with Pesto & Lemon Juice

Time to prepare: 10 min
Time to cook: 30 min
Servings: 2

You will need:

- 2 medium fish fillets of your choice (salmon, cod, trout or other)
- 2 tbsp olive oil
- Salt and pepper to taste
- 4 tbsp Pesto sauce
- 2 tbsp lemon juice

Directions:

1. Preheat the water bath to 135 degrees F.
2. Rub the trout fillets with salt, pepper and pesto sauce, and put the fish and olive oil into the vacuum bag.
3. Seal the bag and set the timer for 30 minutes.
4. Serve sprinkled with lemon juice.

Nutrition per serving:
Calories: 352
Protein: 35 g

Fats: 22 g
Carbs: 1 g

Sea Bass

Time to prepare: 10 min
Time to cook: 30 min
Servings: 2

You will need:

- 2 medium sea bass fillets
- 1 tbsp olive oil
- Salt and pepper to taste
- 1 tbsp lime juice

Directions:

1. Preheat the water bath to 135 degrees F.
2. Rub the sea bass fillets with salt, pepper and olive oil, and put the fish into the vacuum bag.
3. Seal the bag and set the timer for 30 minutes.
4. Serve sprinkled with lime juice.

Nutrition per serving:
Calories: 331
Protein: 30 g
Fats: 20 g
Carbs: 9 g

Garlic & Herbs Cod

Time to prepare: 10 min
Time to cook: 30 min
Servings: 2

You will need:

- 2 medium cod fillets
- 2 garlic cloves, minced
- 1 tbsp fresh rosemary, chopped
- 1 tbsp fresh thyme, chopped
- 2 tbsp unsalted butter
- 1 tbsp olive oil
- Juice of 1 lemon
- Salt and

pepper to taste

Directions:

1. Preheat the water bath to 135 degrees F.
2. Rub the cod fillets with salt and pepper, and put them into the vacuum bag adding rosemary, thyme, butter, minced garlic and lemon juice.
3. Seal the bag and set the timer for 30 minutes.
4. When the time is up, sear the fish in a cast iron skillet in 1 tbsp olive oil on both sides and serve over white rice.

Nutrition per serving: Calories: 250

Protein: 22 g
Fats: 8 g
Carbs: 18 g

Coconut Cream Sea Bass

Time to prepare: 10 min
Time to cook: 30 min
Servings: 2

You will need:

For the fish

- 2 medium cod fillets
- 2 tbsp coconut milk
- Salt and

pepper to taste For
the sauce

- 1/2 cup coconut milk
- 1/2 cup chicken broth
- 1/2 tsp white sugar
- 1 tsp lime juice
- 2 slices ginger root
- Chopped

cilantro for serving

Directions:

1. Preheat the water bath to 135 degrees F.
2. Rub the sea bass fillets with salt, pepper, and coconut milk and put them into the vacuum bag.
3. Seal the bag and set the timer for 30 minutes.
4. While the fish is cooking, make the sauce.

5. Combine the chicken broth and coconut milk in a pan, and simmer for about 10 minutes over the medium heat.

6. Add the lime juice, sugar and ginger root, mix well and take the sauce off the heat. Close the pan with the lid and set aside for a couple of minutes.

7. Put the fish in bowls, pour the sauce over and serve topped with the freshly chopped cilantro.

Nutrition per serving: Calories: 580
Protein: 22 g
Fats: 15 g
Carbs: 88 g

Thai Tom Yum Fish

Time to prepare: 10 min
Time to cook: 30 min
Servings: 2

You will need:

- 2 medium fish fillets (any white fish of your choice)
- 2 tbsp Tom Yum paste
- Fresh cilantro for serving
- 1 tbsp lime juice for serving
-

Directions:

1. Preheat the water bath to 135 degrees F.
2. Rub the fillets with the Tom Yum paste, and put them into the vacuum bag.
3. Seal the bag and set the timer for 30 minutes.
4. Serve over white rice sprinkled with lime juice and topped with freshly chopped cilantro.

Nutrition per serving: Calories: 200
Protein: 20 g
Fats: 5 g
Carbs: 14 g

Chapter 7: Seafood

Butter Shrimps

Time to prepare: 10 min
Time to cook: 25 min
Servings: 4

You will need:

- 16 shrimps, peeled and deveined
- 1 shallot, minced
- 1 tbsp unsalted butter, melted
- 2 tsp thyme
- 1 tsp

lemon zest, grated

Directions:

1. Preheat your cooking machine to 125 degrees F.
2. Put all ingredients in the vacuum bag.
3. Seal the bag, put it into the water bath and set the timer for 25 minutes.
4. Serve immediately as an appetizer or tossed with penne pasta.

Nutrition per serving: Calories:
Protein: g Fats: g Carbs: g

Garlic Shrimps

Time to prepare: 10 min
Time to cook: 25 min
Servings: 4

You will need:

- 16 shrimps, peeled and deveined
- 1 shallot, minced
- 1 tbsp unsalted butter, melted
- 2 garlic

cloves, minced

Directions:

1. Preheat your cooking machine to 125 degrees F.
2. Put all ingredients in the vacuum bag.
3. Seal the bag, put it into the water bath and set the timer for 25 minutes.
4. Serve immediately as an appetizer or tossed with penne pasta.

Nutrition per serving: Calories: 202
Protein: 27 g
Fats: 1 g
Carbs: 9 g

Shrimps Cajun

Time to prepare: 10 min
Time to cook: 25 min
Servings: 4

You will need:

- 16 shrimps, peeled and deveined
- 1 shallot, minced
- 1 tbsp unsalted butter, melted
- 1 tbsp Cajun seasoning
- 2 garlic cloves, minced
- 1 tbsp lemon juice
- Freshly ground black pepper to taste
- 4 tbsp freshly

chopped parsley Directions:

1. Preheat your cooking machine to 125 degrees F.
2. Put all ingredients except parsley into the vacuum bag.
3. Seal the bag, put it into the water bath and set the timer for 25 minutes.
4. Serve immediately as an appetizer garnished with the chopped parsley.

Nutrition per serving: Calories: 133
Protein: 18 g
Fats: 7 g
Carbs: 1 g

Oriental Shrimp Salad

Time to prepare: 10 min
Time to cook: 25 min
Servings: 4

You will need:

For the shrimps

- 16 shrimps, peeled and deveined
- 1 tbsp coconut oil
- 2 garlic cloves, minced
- Salt and

pepper to taste For
the salad

- 1/2 cup sliced shallot
- 1/2 cup

chopped parsley For
the dressing

- 1/2 cup mayo
- 4 tbsp lime juice
- 1 tsp ginger powder
- 1 tsp

curry powder

Directions:

1. Preheat your cooking machine to 125 degrees F.
2. Put shrimp ingredients into the vacuum bag.
3. Seal the bag, put it into the water bath and set the timer for 25

minutes.

4. In the meantime, cook the dressing. Whisk the dressing ingredients together in a bowl.

5. When the shrimps are ready, let them cool down and mix in the dressing, chopped parsley and sliced shallot.

Nutrition per serving: Calories: 363

Protein: 23 g
Fats: 13 g
Carbs: 37 g

Butter Scallops

Time to prepare: 10 min
Time to cook: 30 min
Servings: 4

You will need:
- 16 scallops
- Salt and pepper to taste
- 1 tbsp olive oil
- 1 tbsp butter
- Sous Vide

Hollandaise sauce

Directions:

1. Preheat your cooking machine to 125 degrees F.
2. Remove the muscles from scallops and sprinkle them with salt and pepper.
3. Put the scallops into the vacuum bag, add olive oil.
4. Seal the bag, put it into the water bath and set the timer for 30 minutes.
5. When the scallops are ready, dry them with a paper towel and sear in 1 tbsp butter until golden on both sides.
6. Serve with hollandaise sauce.

Nutrition per serving:
Calories: 215
Protein: 7 g
Fats: 9 g
Carbs: 26 g

Shrimp Penne

Time to prepare: 10 min
Time to cook: 25 min
Servings: 4

You will need:

- 16 shrimps, peeled and deveined
- 1 tbsp lemon zest
- 3 tbsp lemon juice
- Salt and pepper to taste
- 2 tbsp butter
- Cooked penne pasta

for 4 persons Directions:

1. Preheat your cooking machine to 125 degrees F.
2. Put the shrimps into the vacuum bag, add butter and salt and pepper to taste.
3. Seal the bag, put it into the water bath and set the timer for 25 minutes.
4. Carefully pour the cooked shrimps together with all cooking liquid into a medium pot.
5. Add the lemon juice, lemon zest and 2 cups dry white wine to the pot.
6. Simmer the mixture until it thickens, pour the sauce over

the cooked penne and serve.

Nutrition per serving: Calories: 450
Protein: 19 g
Fats: 17 g
Carbs: 55 g

Lobster Provencal

Time to prepare: 10 min
Time to cook: 1 h
Servings: 4

You will need:

- 4 lobster tails
- 10 tbsp butter
- 2 tbsp Provencal herbs
- Salt and pepper to taste
- 4 tbsp lemon

juice for serving

Directions:

1. Preheat your cooking machine to 135 degrees F.
2. Remove the shell from the lobster tails; sprinkle them with salt and pepper, season evenly with herbs.
3. Put the tails into the vacuum bag, add butter and seal the bag.
4. Set the timer for 1 hour.
5. Drizzle the cooked lobster tails with the cooking liquid, sprinkle each with 1 tbsp lemon juice and serve.

Nutrition per serving: Calories: 260
Protein: 21 g
Fats: 16 g
Carbs: 8 g

Blue Cheese Lobster Tails

Time to prepare: 10 min
Time to cook: 1 h
Servings: 4

You will need:

- 4 lobster tails, shells removed
- 10 tbsp butter
- Salt and pepper to taste
- Sous Vide Blue Cheese

sauce for serving Directions:

1. Preheat your cooking machine to 135 degrees F.
2. Sprinkle the lobster tails with salt and pepper.
3. Put the tails into the vacuum bag and add the butter.
4. Seal the bag and set the timer for 1 hour.
5. Drizzle the cooked lobster tails with the cooking liquid and serve with Sous Vide Blue Cheese sauce.

Nutrition per serving: Calories: 260
Protein: 21 g
Fats: 16 g
Carbs: 8 g

Lobster Roll

Time to prepare: 10 min
Time to cook: 1 h
Servings: 4

You will need:

- 2 lobster tails, shells removed
- 2 tbsp butter
- Salt and pepper to taste
- 4 tbsp mayo
- 1 tbsp lemon juice
- 4 big salad leaves
- 4

hot dog
buns

Directions:

1. Preheat your cooking machine to 135 degrees F.
2. Sprinkle the lobster tails with salt and pepper.
3. Put the tails into the vacuum bag and add the butter.
4. Seal the bag and set the timer for 1 hour.
5. When the time is up, carefully remove the cooked lobster tails, let them cool down a bit and chop them into bite-size pieces.
6. Mix the lobster pieces with mayo, sprinkle with lemon juice.

7. Put 1 big salad leave into each hot dog bun, lay the lobster mayo mixture on each leave and serve.

Nutrition per serving: Calories: 260
Protein: 21 g
Fats: 16 g
Carbs: 8 g

Lobster Cajun Spaghetti

Time to prepare: 10 min
Time to cook: 25 min
Servings: 4

You will need:

- 2 lobster tails, shell removed
- 1 shallot, minced
- 1 tbsp unsalted butter, melted
- 1 tbsp Cajun seasoning
- 2 garlic cloves, minced
- 4 tbsp lemon juice
- 1 tbsp lemon zest
- Salt and pepper to taste
- 2 cups dry white wine
- 4 tbsp freshly chopped parsley
- Cooked spaghetti

(for 4 persons) Directions:

1. Preheat your cooking machine to 135 degrees F.
2. Season the lobster tails with Cajun, salt and pepper, and put into the vacuum bag. Add shallots and butter.
3. Seal the bag, put it into the water bath and set the timer for 1 hour.
4. Carefully chop the cooked lobster tails into bite- size pieces and pour them together with all cooking

liquid into a medium pot.

5. Add the lemon juice, lemon zest and 2 cups dry white wine to the pot.

6. Simmer the mixture until it thickens, pour the sauce over the cooked penne and serve with chopped fresh parsley.

Nutrition per serving: Calories: 450
Protein: 19 g
Fats: 17 g
Carbs: 55 g

Aromatic Shrimps

Time to prepare: 10 min
Time to cook: 30 min
Servings: 2

You will need:

- 1 pound large shrimps, peeled and deveined
- 1 tsp olive oil
- Any aromatics of your choice
- Salt to taste
- 2 tbsp lemon juice(optional)

Directions:

1. Preheat your cooking machine to 125 degrees F.
2. Season the shrimps with salt and put into the vacuum bag.
3. Add 1 tsp olive oil and aromatics.
4. Seal the bag, put it into the water bath and set the timer for 30 minutes.
5. Serve with any sauce of your choice or sprinkled with lemon juice.

Nutrition per serving: Calories: 202
Protein: 27g
Fats: 1 g
Carbs: 9 g

Drunken Mussels

Time to prepare: 10 min
Time to cook: 15 min
Servings: 2

You will need:

- 2 pounds mussels in their shells
- 1 cup dry white wine
- 2 garlic cloves, chopped
- 4 tbsp butter
- S

alt to
taste

Directio
ns:

1. Preheat your cooking machine to 194 degrees F.
2. Season the mussels with salt and put into the vacuum bag.
3. Reduce the air in the bag to 30% (70% of vacuum) otherwise the shell won't open.
4. Add dry white wine, garlic cloves and butter
5. Seal the bag, put it into the water bath and set the timer for 15 minutes.
6. Serve sprinkled with lemon juice.

Nutrition per serving:
Calories: 370
Protein: 18 g
Fats: 25 g
Carbs: 18 g

Garlic Squid

Time to prepare: 10 min
Time to cook: 2 h
Servings: 4

You will need:

- 4 small clean squids
- 2 garlic cloves, chopped
- 2 tbsp olive oil
- Salt and

pepper to taste

Directions:

1. Preheat your cooking machine to 140 degrees F.
2. Season the squid with salt and put into the vacuum bag.
3. Add olive oil and chopped garlic
4. Seal the bag, put it into the water bath and cook for 2 hours.
5. Serve sprinkled

with lemon juice.

Nutrition per serving:
Calories: 170
Protein: 19 g
Fats: 7 g
Carbs: 8 g

Hong Kong Style Squid with Teriyaki Sauce

Time to prepare: 10 min
Time to cook: 2 h
Servings: 4

You will need:

- 4 small clean squids
- 2 garlic cloves, chopped
- 4 tbsp olive oil
- 4 tbsp Teriyaki sauce
- 1 tbsp sesame seeds
- Salt and

pepper to taste

Directions:

1. Preheat your cooking machine to 140 degrees F.
2. Season the squid with salt and put into the vacuum bag.
3. Add 2 tbsp olive oil and chopped garlic
4. Seal the bag, put it into the water bath and cook for 2 hours.
5. Preheat 2 tbsp olive oil in the skillet, pour the Teriyaki sauce and sear the squids on medium to high heat from both sides until brown.

6. Serve sprinkled with
sesame seeds.

Nutrition per serving:
Calories: 170
Protein: 19 g
Fats: 7 g
Carbs: 8 g

Seafood Mix with Tomato, Wine and Parsley

Time to prepare: 10 min
Time to cook: 2 h
Servings: 4

You will need:

- 2 pounds seafood mix, thawed
- 1 cup tomatoes in own juice, diced
- 1/2 cup dry white wine
- 1 bay leaf
- 1 tsp dried oregano
- 2 garlic cloves, minced
- 2 tbsp olive oil
- Salt and pepper to taste
- Lemon juice for sprinkling
- Chopped parsley

for sprinkling Directions:

1. Preheat your cooking machine to 140 degrees F.
2. Sprinkle the thawed seafood mix with salt and pepper and put it into the vacuum bag adding tomatoes, bay leaf, dried oregano, garlic, olive oil and white wine.
3. Seal the bag, put it into the water bath and cook for 2 hours.
4. Serve over rice sprinkled with freshly chopped parsley and

lemon juice.

Nutrition per serving: Calories: 370
Protein: 18 g
Fats: 25 g
Carbs: 18 g

Chapter 8: Chicken

Curry Chicken & Bacon Wraps

Time to prepare: 10 min
Time to cook: 7 h
Servings: 6

You will need:

- 4 pounds bacon, sliced
- 8 pound chicken breast, cut into 6 pieces
- 1 tbsp unsalted butter
- 1 tbsp ground curry
- 2 tbsp lemon juice
- Salt and

pepper to taste

Directions:

1. Preheat your Sous Vide machine to 160 degrees F
2. Season the chicken pieces with curry, salt and pepper.
3. Wrap each piece in sliced bacon, sprinkling each with fresh lemon juice.
4. Carefully put the pieces into the vacuum bag.
5. Seal the bag removing the air as much as possible and set the cooking time for 7 hours.

6. Serve warm.

Nutrition per serving: Calories: 210
Protein: 9 g
Fats: 13 g
Carbs: 18 g

Honey Turkey & Bacon Wraps

Time to prepare: 10 min
Time to cook: 7 h
Servings: 6

You will need:

- 4 pounds bacon, sliced
- 8 pound turkey fillet, cut into 6 pieces
- 1 tbsp unsalted butter
- 1 tbsp ground paprika
- 2 tbsp oregano
- 1 tbsp liquid honey
- 2 tbsp lemon juice
- Salt and

pepper to taste

Directions:

1. Preheat your Sous Vide machine to 160 degrees F
2. Season the turkey slices with paprika, oregano, salt and pepper.
3. Wrap each piece in sliced bacon, sprinkling each with honey and fresh lemon juice.
4. Carefully put the wraps into the vacuum bag.
5. Seal the bag removing the air as much as possible and set the cooking time for 7 hours.

6. Serve warm.

Nutrition per serving: Calories: 210
Protein: 9 g
Fats: 13 g
Carbs: 18 g

Chicken Meatballs with Herbs and Tomato Sauce

Time to prepare: 10 min
Time to cook: 2 h
Servings: 6

You will need:

- 8 pounds ground chicken
- 1 tbsp unsalted butter
- 2 tbsp tomato sauce
- 3 tbsp dried oregano
- 1 big egg
- Salt and

pepper to taste

Directions:

1. Preheat your Sous Vide machine to 142 degrees F.
2. In a big bowl, combine the ground chicken with egg, butter, salt, pepper and oregano. Mix well until even.
3. Make 6 meatballs.
4. Carefully put the balls into the vacuum bag and add the tomato sauce.
5. Seal the bag removing the air as much as possible, put it into the water bath and set the cooking time for 2 hours.

6. Serve warm with white rice or mashed potato.

Nutrition per serving:
Calories: 214
Protein: 17 g
Fats: 14 g
Carbs: 4 g

Turkey Curry Meatballs

Time to prepare: 10 min
Time to cook: 2 hours
Servings: 6

You will need:

- 8 pounds ground turkey
- 1 tbsp unsalted butter
- 2 tbsp curry powder
- 1 big egg
- Salt and pepper to taste
- Chopped

parsley for serving

Directions:

1. Preheat your Sous Vide machine to 142 degrees F.
2. In a big bowl, combine the ground turkey with egg, butter, salt, pepper and curry powder. Mix well until even.
3. Make 6 meatballs.
4. Carefully put the balls into the vacuum bag.
5. Seal the bag removing the air as much as possible, put it into the water bath and set the cooking time for 2 hours.
6. Serve warm with white rice garnished with freshly

chopped parsley.

Nutrition per serving: Calories: 214
Protein: 17 g
Fats: 14 g
Carbs: 4 g

Duck Leg Confit

Time to prepare: 10-12 hours
Time to cook: 12 h 10 min
Servings: 2

You will need:

- 2 duck legs
- 1 tbsp dried thyme
- 2 big bay leaves, crushed
- 6 tbsp duck fat
- Salt and pepper to taste
- Cranberry

sauce for serving

Directions:

1. Preheat your Sous Vide machine to 167 degrees F.
2. Mix the bay leaves with salt, pepper and thyme, and season the duck legs with the mixture.
3. Refrigerate overnight.
4. In the morning, rinse the legs with cold water and carefully put them into the vacuum bag.
5. Add 4 tbsp duck fat, seal the bag removing the air as much as possible, put it into the water bath and set the cooking time for 12 hours.
6. Before serving, roast the legs in 2 remaining tbsp of duck fat until

crispy.

7. Serve with cranberry sauce.

Nutrition per serving:
Calories: 470
Protein: 34 g
Fats: 37 g
Carbs: 15 g

Caramelized Chicken Teriyaki

Time to prepare: 10 min
Time to cook: 1 h 40 min
Servings: 2

You will need:

- 2 chicken fillets
- 1 tbsp ginger juice
- 3 tsp sugar
- 1/2 tsp salt
- 2 tbsp Japanese Sake
- 2 tbsp

unsweetened soy sauce

Directions:

1. In a small bowl, mix the ginger juice with salt and 1 tsp sugar.
2. Rub the chicken and leave it overnight to marinate.
3. In the morning, carefully put the chicken into the vacuum bag and preheat your sous vide machine to 140 degrees F.
4. Seal the bag removing the air as much as possible, put it into the water bath and set the cooking time for 1 hour 30 minutes.
5. Mix 2 tsp sugar with sake and soy sauce and boil in a small skillet or saucepan until the sauce thickens a

bit.

6. Pour half of the sauce over the cooked chicken breasts and torch the glaze until it caramelizes.

7. Chop the fillets and serve over white rice, drizzling with the remaining liquid half of the sauce.

Nutrition per serving: Calories: 490
Protein: 58 g
Fats: 18 g
Carbs: 32 g

Simple Chicken Breast

Time to prepare: 10 min
Time to cook: 3 h
Servings: 2

You will need:
- 2 chicken breast fillets
- 2 tbsp unsalted butter
- Salt and pepper to taste
- 1 garlic
clove, halved

Directions:
1. Preheat your sous vide machine to 145 degrees F.
2. Carefully put the chicken breasts into the vacuum bag. Add the butter, salt, pepper and halved garlic cloves and seal the bag removing the air as much as possible.
3. Put it into the water bath and set the cooking time for 3 hours.
4. Serve with any siding and sauces of your choice. This is a really basic recipe, so practically everything will work amazingly!

Nutrition per serving: Calories: 171
Protein: 32 g
Fats: 4 g
Carbs: 0.2 g

Chicken Breast with Lemon and French Herbs

Time to prepare: 10 min
Time to cook: 3 h 20 min
Servings: 2

You will need:

- 2 chicken breast fillets
- Salt and pepper to taste
- 1

tsp olive
oil For the
sauce:

- 1 onion, sliced
- 2 garlic cloves, minced
- 1 tbsp olive oil
- 1 tbsp unsalted butter
- 1 cup button mushrooms, coarsely chopped
- 2 tbsp white wine
- 1/2 cup chicken broth
- 1 cup cream
- Salt and

pepper to taste
Directions:

1. Preheat your sous vide machine to 145 degrees F.
2. Carefully put the chicken breasts into the vacuum bag. Add the

butter, salt, pepper and halved garlic cloves and seal the bag removing the air as much as possible.

3. Put it into the water bath and set the cooking time for 3 hours.
4. While the chicken is cooking, make the sauce.
5. Heat olive oil in a medium skillet, and cook the chopped onion for about 2-3 minutes.

6. Add the butter and minced garlic and cook for 2 more minutes.
7. Add the chopped mushrooms and cook at the medium heat until the liquid evaporates.
8. Add the white wine, cook until the liquid almost evaporates and add the chicken broth and cream.
9. Continue cooking until the sauce thickens, add salt and pepper if needed. Set the sauce aside.
10. Remove the cooked chicken from the sous vide machine and roast it in a skillet on both sides until light brown. Add the sauce and wait just till it heats to the desired temperature.
11. Serve with mashed potato.

Nutrition per serving:
Calories: 171
Protein: 32 g
Fats: 4 g
Carbs: 0.2 g

Chicken Breast with Mushroom Sauce

Time to prepare: 10 min
Time to cook: 3 h 20 min
Servings: 2

You will need:
- 2 chicken breast fillets
- 2 tbsp lemon juice
- Salt and pepper to taste
- French herbs seasoning to taste
- 1 tsp olive oil
- 1 tsp butter Directions:

1. In a small saucepan, mix the olive oil with the lemon juice and the herbs and set aside for an hour to marinate.
2. Preheat your sous vide machine to 145 degrees F.
3. Carefully put the chicken breasts into the vacuum bag and seal it removing the air as much as possible.
4. Put it into the water bath and set the cooking time for 3 hours.
5. Heat 1 tsp butter in a frying pan and sear the cooked fillets for about 1 minute on each side until golden.

Nutrition per serving: Calories: 235
Protein: 29 g
Fats: 8 g
Carbs: 11 g

Italian Chicken Marsala

Time to prepare: 10 min
Time to cook: 2 h 20 min
Servings: 2

You will need:

- 4 chicken breast fillets, bones and skin removed
- Salt and pepper to taste
- 1 cup all-purpose flour
- 1 tbsp olive oil
- 1 pound porcini mushrooms, chopped
- 1 cup dry red wine
- 1 cup chicken broth
- 3 tbsp freshly

chopped parsley Directions:

1. Preheat your sous vide machine to 140 degrees F.
2. Carefully put the chicken breasts sprinkled with salt and pepper into the vacuum bag, and seal it removing the air as much as possible.
3. Put it into the water bath and set the cooking time for 2 hours.
4. When the time is up, remove the chicken breasts from the bag, dry them with kitchen towels and dredge them in the flour.

5. Heat olive oil in cast iron skillet and brown the fillets over the medium heat until golden. Set aside.

6. Put the chopped mushrooms in the skillet and saute for 5 minutes. Add the wine and chicken broth, simmer for 10 minutes.

7. Pour the sauce over the chicken breasts and serve sprinkled with the freshly chopped parsley.

Nutrition per serving: Calories: 353
Protein: 34 g
Fats: 12 g
Carbs: 15 g

Chapter 9. Lamb

Lamb Shank Cooked in Red Wine

Time to prepare: 10 min
Time to cook: 48 h
Servings: 10

You will need:

- 1 lamb shank
- 2 sprigs thyme
- 2 tbsp olive oil
- 1/2 cup dry red wine
- Salt and

pepper to taste

Directions:

1. Preheat the water bath to 144 degrees F.
2. Sprinkle the lamb shank with salt and pepper. Put it into the vacuum bag together with other ingredients and seal it.
3. Set the cooking timer for 48 hours.
4. Serve with mashed potato, pouring 3-4 tbsp of cooking juices over before serving.

Nutrition per serving: Calories: 673
Protein: 34 g
Fats: 38 g
Carbs: 18 g

Lamb Chops with Honey Mustard Sauce

Time to prepare: 10 min
Time to cook: 3 h 10 min
Servings: 4

You will need:

For the lamb

- 4 lamb chops
- 4 rosemary sprigs
- 4 tbsp olive oil
- Salt and

pepper to taste For
the sauce

- 4 tbsp Dijon Mustard
- 1 tsp liquid honey
- 1

tbsp lemon
juice

Directions:

1. Preheat your Sous Vide machine to 145 degrees F.
2. Season the lamb shank with salt and pepper.
3. Put the lamb into the bag, add 2 tbsp olive oil and 1 rosemary sprig on each chop.
4. Remove the air and cook for 3 hours.
5. When the time is up, preheat the remaining 2 tbsp olive oil in a cast

iron skillet and sear the chops over high heat for about 30 seconds on each side until golden.

6. Whisk the mustard with liquid honey and lemon juice, pour the sauce over the chops and serve.

Nutrition per serving: Calories: 301
Protein: 20 g
Fats: 22 g
Carbs: 5 g

Lamb Shank with Wine Sauce and Rosemary

Time to prepare: 10 min
Time to cook: 48 h
Servings: 10

You will need:

- 1 lamb shank
- 2 sprigs rosemary
- 2 tbsp olive oil
- 1/2 cup dry red wine
- Salt and

pepper to taste

Directions:

1. Preheat the water bath to 144 degrees F.
2. Sprinkle the lamb shank with salt and pepper. Put the lamb, rosemary, olive oil into the vacuum bag and seal it.
3. Set the cooking timer for 48 hours.
4. When the time is up, carefully open the bag and pour the cooking juices into a pan.
5. Bring the sauces to boil and remove the scums from the top of the liquid with a spoon.
6. Add the red wine and simmer until the liquid reduces to the

sauce.

7. Pour the sauce over the lamb, the siding and serve.

Nutrition per serving: Calories: 673
Protein: 34 g
Fats: 38 g
Carbs: 18 g

Lamb Shoulder

Time to prepare: 10 min
Time to cook: 8 h
Servings: 10

You will need:

- 2 pounds lamb shoulder, bones removed
- 1 garlic clove
- 2 tbsp olive oil
- 2 rosemary sprigs
- Salt and

pepper to taste

Directions:

1. Preheat the water bath to 180 degrees F.
2. Season the lamb shank with salt and pepper.
3. Put the lamb into the vacuum bag, adding rosemary sprigs, olive oil and garlic.
4. Seal the bag.
5. Set the cooking timer for 8 hours.
6. Serve with boiled potatoes pouring the cooking juices over.

Nutrition per serving: Calories: 230
Protein: 20 g
Fats: 13 g
Carbs: 7 g

Sliced Lamb Shoulder with Jalapeno Sauce

Time to prepare: 10 min
Time to cook: 8 h
Servings: 10

You will need:

- 2 pounds lamb shoulder, bones removed
- 1 garlic clove
- 2 tbsp olive oil
- Salt and pepper to taste
- Sous Vide

Jalapeno Sauce

Directions:

1. Preheat the water bath to 180 degrees F.
2. Season the lamb shank with salt and pepper.
3. Put the lamb into the vacuum bag, adding olive oil and garlic.
4. Seal the bag.
5. Set the cooking timer for 8 hours.
6. Slices the cooked shoulder and serve it with the Sous Vide jalapeno sauce.

Nutrition per serving: Calories: 230
Protein: 20 g
Fats: 13 g
Carbs: 7 g

Plain Lamb Shank with Cranberry Sauce

Time to prepare: 10 min
Time to cook: 48 h
Servings: 10

You will need:

- 1 lamb shank
- 2 tbsp olive oil
- 2 garlic cloves, coarsely chopped
- Salt and pepper to taste
- Sous Vide

cranberry sauce

Directions:

1. Preheat the water bath to 144 degrees F.
2. Sprinkle the lamb shank with salt and pepper. Put it into the vacuum bag together with olive oil and garlic.
3. Seal the bag.
4. Set the cooking time for 48 hours.
5. Serve with boiled potato and Sous Vide cranberry sauce.

Nutrition per serving:
Calories: 230
Protein: 20 g
Fats: 13 g
Carbs: 7 g

Leg of Lamb with Smoked Paprika

Time to prepare: 10 min
Time to cook: 10 h 20 min
Servings: 6

You will need:

- 3 pounds lamb leg, bones removed
- 2 garlic cloves
- 1 tsp ground smoked paprika
- 2 tbsp dried oregano
- 1 garlic clove, minced
- 2 tbsp olive oil
- Salt and pepper to taste
- Ju

ice of 1
lemon

Directions:

1. Preheat your Sous Vide machine to 134 degrees F.
2. Prepare the seasoning: whisk together the minced garlic, olive oil, smoked paprika, salt, pepper and oregano.
3. Spread the mixture evenly over the lamb.
4. Put the lamb into the bag, remove the air and cook for 10 hours.
5. When the time is up, place the lamb under the preheated grill

for 4-5 minutes just until it becomes crispy.

6. Slice the cooked lamb and serve it sprinkled with lemon juice.

Nutrition per serving: Calories: 230
Protein: 20 g
Fats: 13 g
Carbs: 7 g

Garlic & Butter Lamb Chops

Time to prepare: 10 min
Time to cook: 3 h 20 min
Servings: 4

You will need:
For the lamb

- 4 lamb chops
- 4 thyme sprigs
- 2 tbsp olive oil
- Salt and

pepper to taste For
searing

- 2 tbsp butter, melted
- 1 garlic

clove, minced
Directions:

1. Preheat your Sous Vide machine to 145 degrees F.
2. Season the lamb shank with salt and pepper.
3. Put the lamb into the bag; add 2 tbsp olive oil and 1 thyme sprig on each chop.
4. Remove the air and cook for 3 hours.
5. When the time is up, combine the melted butter with the minced garlic, and coat each cooked chop with the butter-garlic mixture.

6. Sear each chop in the preheated cast iron skillet for 20 seconds on each side until golden.

Nutrition per serving: Calories: 230
Protein: 20 g
Fats: 13 g
Carbs: 7 g

Party Lamb Dips with Lime

Time to prepare: 3 h
Time to cook: 6 h 10 min
Servings: 4

You will need:
For the lamb

- 10 lamb short ribs
- Zest of 1 lime
- Juice of 1 lime
- 2 garlic cloves, minced
- 4 tbsp olive oil
- Salt and pepper to taste
- 2 tbsp

ground paprika For
the sauce

- Any preferred

Sous Vide sauce Directions:

1. Whisk together the lime juice,
   lime zest, minced garlic, olive oil,
   salt and pepper.
2. Rub the mixture into the ribs
   and leave for 2-3 hours to
   marinate.
3. Preheat your Sous Vide machine to
   174 degrees F.
4. Put the lamb in the bag
   together with the
   marinade

5. Seal the bag and set the timer for 6 hours.
6. 30 minutes before the time is up, preheat the oven to 428 degrees F.
7. Cook the ribs in the preheated oven for 5 minutes until crispy.
8. Serve on a plate with any preferred Sous Vide sauce.

Nutrition per serving: Calories: 230
Protein: 20 g
Fats: 13 g
Carbs: 7 g

Glazed Lamb Leg

Time to prepare: 10 min
Time to cook: 24 h
Servings: 4

You will need:

- 1 lamb leg
- 2 tbsp tomato paste
- 2 cups balsamic vinegar
- 4 garlic cloves
- 4 thyme sprigs
- Salt and

pepper to taste

Directions:

1. Preheat your Sous Vide machine to 167 degrees F.
2. Combine the vinegar and tomato paste in a medium pan and reduce the mixture until thick over the medium heat.
3. Rub salt and pepper into the leg, pour the sauce over it.
4. Put the leg into the vacuum bag.
5. Add thyme and garlic cloves
6. Seal the bag and set the timer for 24 hours.
7. When the time is up, carefully open the bag, remove the leg and pour the cooking juices into a pan.

8. Reduce the liquid over medium heat until thick, mixing it carefully with a spoon and making sure it does not burn.

9. Pour the sauce over the leg and serve.

Nutrition per serving:
Calories: 239

Protein: 17 g
Fats: 23 g
Carbs: 10 g

Chapter 10. Beef

Beef Tenderloin

Time to prepare: 10 min
Time to cook: 2 h 10 min
Servings: 1

You will need:
- 1 beef tenderloin
- 2 garlic cloves, minced
- 1/2 tbsp dried rosemary
- 1/2 tbsp dried thyme
- 1 tbsp olive oil
- Salt and pepper to taste Directions:
    1. Preheat your cooking machine to 133 degrees F.
    2. Season the meat with salt and pepper to taste. Then grease it with the olive oil on both sides and add the herbs.
    3. Carefully place the meat into the vacuum bag.
    4. Seal the bag and set the cooking time for 2 hours.
    5. Remove the meat from the bag, dry it setting the oily herbs and garlic mixture from the bag.
    6. Heat 1 tbsp olive oil in the skillet and roast the cooked piece of meat

for about 1 minute on each side.

7.   Serve hot garnished with the reserved mixture Nutrition per serving:

Calories: 276

Protein: 20 g

Fats: 21 g

Carbs: 0 g

Striploin Steak

Time to prepare: 10 min
Time to cook: 1 h 10 min
Servings: 1

You will need:

- 1 strip steak
- 2 garlic cloves, minced
- 1/2 tbsp dried rosemary
- 1/2 tbsp dried thyme
- 1 tbsp olive oil
- Salt and

pepper to taste

Directions:

1. Preheat your cooking machine to 129 degrees F.
2. Season the strip steak with salt and pepper to taste. Then grease it with the olive oil on both sides and add the herbs.
3. Put the steak into a plastic bag removing as much air as possible.
4. Seal it and set the cooking time for 1 hour.
5. Remove the meat from the bag, dry it setting the oily herbs and garlic mixture from the bag.
6. Heat 1 tbsp olive oil in the skillet and roast the cooked piece of meat for about 1 minute on each side.
7. Serve hot garnished with the reserved

mixture.

Nutrition per serving: Calories: 225
Protein: 23g
Fats: 10 g
Carbs: 0 g

Beef Burgers

Time to prepare: 10 min
Time to cook: 1 h 10 min
Servings: 1

You will need:
- 10 pounds minced beef
- 2 buns for hamburgers
- 2 slice Cheddar cheese
- 8 slices marinated cucumbers
- 2 tbsp Dijon mustard
- 2 tbsp ketchup
- Salt and

pepper to taste

Directions:

1. Preheat your cooking machine to 137 degrees F.
2. Shape the minced beef into 2 putties, seasoning them with salt and pepper to taste.
3. Put them into a plastic bag removing as much air as possible.
4. Seal it and set the cooking time for 1 hour.
5. While the patties are cooking, toast the burger buns.
6. Remove the patties from the bag, dry them and roast on high heat for about 20-30 seconds on each

side.

7. Assemble the burgers with Cheddar slices, mustard and ketchup and sliced marinated cucumbers and serve.

Nutrition per serving: Calories: 280
Protein: 22 g

Fats: 20 g
Carbs: 40 g

Ribeye Steak in Mushroom Sauce

Time to prepare: 10 min
Time to cook: 2 h 10 min
Servings: 1

You will need:

- 1 ribeye steak
- 1/2 tbsp dried rosemary
- 1 tbsp olive oil
- Salt and
pepper to taste

Directions:

1. Preheat your Sous Vide machine to 129 degrees F.
2. Season the ribeye steak with salt and pepper to taste. Then grease it with the olive oil on both sides and add the dried rosemary.
3. Put the steak into a plastic bag removing as much air as possible.
4. Place the bag into the water bath and set the cooking time for 2 hours.
5. Remove the meat from the bag, dry it and sear for about 1 minute on each side.
6. Serve hot with mashed potato and mushroom sauce.

Nutrition per serving: Calories: 290

Protein: 25 g
Fats: 30 g
Carbs: 3 g

Butter Steak

Time to prepare: 10 min
Time to cook: 1 h 10 min
Servings: 1

You will need:

- 1 strip steak
- 1 tbsp olive oil
- Salt and pepper to taste
- 1 tbsp unsalted butter
- 1 bay leaf

Directions:

1. Preheat your cooking machine to 129 degrees F.
2. Season the strip steak with salt and pepper to taste. Then grease it with the olive oil on both sides.
3. Put the steak into a plastic bag, add the bay leaf and remove as much air as possible.
4. Seal it and set the cooking time for 1 hour.
5. Remove the steak from the bag and dry it with paper towels.
6. Heat 1 tbsp butter in the skillet

and wait till it stops bubbling.

7.   Roast the steak for about 1 minute on each side. Nutrition per serving:

Calories: 210
Protein: 25 g
Fats: 16g
Carbs: 34 g

Meatballs with Herbs and Tomato Sauce

Time to prepare: 20 min
Time to cook: 2 h
Servings: 6

You will need:

- 8 pounds minced beef
- 1 garlic clove, minced
- 1 shallot, finely sliced
- 2 tbsp coriander
- 3 tbsp dried oregano
- 1 big egg
- 2 tbsp cranberry sauce
- Salt and

pepper to taste

Directions:

1. Preheat your Sous Vide machine to 142 degrees F.
2. In a big bowl, combine the minced beef with egg, garlic, shallot, oregano, egg, salt and pepper. Mix well until even.
3. Make 6 meatballs.
4. Carefully put the balls into the vacuum bag.
5. Seal the bag removing the air as much as possible, put it into the water bath and set the cooking time for 2 hours.

6. Serve warm with cranberry sauce.

Nutrition per serving:
Calories: 283
Protein: 30 g
Fats: 13 g
Carbs: 11 g

Pumpkin Meatballs

Time to prepare: 20 min
Time to cook: 2 h
Servings: 6

You will need:

- 1/2 cup fresh pumpkin, grated
- 8 pounds minced beef
- 1 garlic clove, minced
- 1 shallot, finely sliced
- 1 big egg
- Salt and

pepper to taste

Directions:

1. Preheat your Sous Vide machine to 142 degrees F.
2. In a big bowl, combine the minced beef with the grated pumpkin, egg, garlic, shallot, salt and pepper. Mix well until even.
3. Make 6 meatballs.
4. Carefully put the balls into the vacuum bag.
5. Seal the bag removing the air as much as possible, put it into the water bath and set the cooking time for 2 hours.
6. Serve warm with a preferred sauce.

Nutrition per serving:
Calories: 283
Protein: 30 g
Fats: 13 g
Carbs: 11 g

Veal Cheeks in Red Wine

Time to prepare: 20 min
Time to cook: 8 h 10 min
Servings: 6

You will need:

- 4 veal cheeks
- 1 shallot, finely sliced
- 2 celery sticks, diced
- 2 cups meat broth
- 1 carrot, diced
- 1 tsp dried basil
- 2 tbsp liquid honey
- 1 cup tomatoes in own juice, crushed
- 1 tbsp olive oil
- Salt and

pepper to taste

Directions:

1. Preheat your Sous Vide machine to 78 degrees F.
2. Season the cheeks with salt and paper and place them in the vacuum bag.
3. Heat the olive oil in the saucepan and saute shallot, carrot, celery and garlic for 3 minutes.
4. Add the red wine and cook until the liquid almost evaporates.

5. Add the crushed tomatoes and meat broth, and cook until the liquid is reduced by half.
6. When the sauce cools down, add it to the vacuum bag and seal it, removing the air.
7. Cook in the preheated water bath for 8 hours.
8. Serve hot over the baked potato.

Nutrition per serving:

Calories: 350
Protein: 15 g
Fats: 24 g
Carbs: 13 g

Beef Stroganoff

Time to prepare: 20 min
Time to cook: 1 h 20 min
Servings: 2

You will need:

- 1 1/2 pounds beef loin
- 6 tbsp unsalted butter
- 1 cup button mushrooms, chopped
- 1 onion, finale chopped
- 3 tbsp all-purpose flour
- 1 cup beef broth
- 2 tbsp dry white wine
- 1 cup sour cream
- Ro
semary sprigs

Directions:

1. Preheat your Sous Vide machine to 136 degrees F.
2. Season the steaks with salt and paper and place them in the vacuum bag, putting a piece of butter and rosemary sprigs on top of each steak.
3. Seal the bag and cook the steaks in the preheated water bath for 1 hour.
4. In the meantime, heat 2 tbsp butter in a skillet and saute the chopped

onion until translucent.

5. Add the mushrooms, salt and pepper to taste, and cook until the liquid evaporates. Set aside.

6. Sear the steaks in 1 tbsp butter. Set aside.

7. Add 2 tbsp butter and flour to the pan, mix it well with a spoon, add the stock, wine and cooked mushrooms.

8. Cook until the sauce thickens. Stir in the sour cream and serve the sauce with the chopped steak over mashed potato.

Nutrition per serving: Calories: 361
Protein: 35 g
Fats: 16 g
Carbs: 17 g

Beef Bourguignon

Time to prepare: 20 min
Time to cook: 24 h + 1 h
Servings: 4

You will need:

- 1 1/2 pounds beef chunks
- 2 tbsp cornstarch
- 2 carrots, peeled and chopped
- 1 onion, peeled and sliced
- 2 garlic cloves, minced
- 1 cup water
- 1 tbsp beef stock
- 1 tbsp tomato paste
- 1 tsp dried thyme
- 1 bay leaf
- 4 tbsp unsalted butter
- 1 cup button mushrooms, chopped
- 2 tbsp flour
- 1

bottle dry red
wine Directions:

1. Season the beef chunks with salt, pepper and cornstarch, tossing it gently to make sure the chunks are evenly coated. Put the chunks in the vacuum bag.
2. In a large skillet, heat the olive oil and sear the chunks for about 3

minutes until lightly browned.
Transfer the beef to the vacuum
bag.

3. Add carrot, garlic and onion to
   the skillet, add salt to taste and
   cook for about 10 minutes,

stirring occasionally. Add the vegetables to the vacuum bag.

4. Finally, add a bottle of wine, tomato paste, beef broth and dried thyme to the bag, seal it and cook for 24 hours in the water bath preheated to 140 degrees F.

5. Heat a large skillet, combine 2 tbsp butter with the flour to form the paste.

6. Carefully open the bag and add the liquid to the paste, mixing well to avoid lumps. Simmer for about 5 minutes.

7. Add everything that is left in the bag, mix well with a spatula and serve over mashed potatoes or cauliflower puree.

Nutrition per serving: Calories: 461
Protein: 34 g
Fats: 17 g
Carbs: 11 g

Chapter 11. Pork

Roasted Sausages

Time to prepare: 10 min
Time to cook: 3 h 10 min
Servings: 4

You will need:

- 1 pound pork sausages
- 1/2 tsp ground paprika
- 1/4 tsp ground chili
- 1 tsp oregano
- 1 tsp turmeric powder
- 1/2 tsp chili pepper
- 1 tbsp unsalted butter
- Salt and

pepper to taste

Directions:

1. Preheat your cooking machine to 155 degrees F.
2. Season the sausages with spices, making sure the sausages are evenly covered with spices.
3. Place the ingredients in the vacuum bag.
4. Seal it, setting the timer for 3 hours.
5. Melt 1 tbsp butter in the preheated skillet and roast each sausage until golden.

6. Serve hot.

Nutrition per serving: Calories: 300
Protein: 19 g
Fats: 25 g
Carbs: 3 g

Ginger & Parsley Ham

Time to prepare: 10 min
Time to cook: 9 h
Servings: 4

You will need:

- 2 pounds ham, sliced
- 1/2 tsp ground ginger
- 1 tsp sage
- 1 tbsp dried parsley
- 2 tbsp olive oil
- Salt and

pepper to taste

Directions:

1. Preheat your cooking machine to 145 degrees F.
2. In a small bowl, mix the olive oil with spices.
3. Season the ham slices with the oil mixture, making sure the slices are evenly covered with it.
4. Place the ingredients in the vacuum bag.
5. Seal it, setting the timer for 9 hours.

Serve immediately.

Nutrition per serving: Calories: 220
Protein: 30 g
Fats: 9 g
Carbs: 4 g

Japanese Style Pork Chops

Time to prepare: 5 min
Time to cook: 1 h 30 min
Servings: 2

You will need:

- 2 pork rib chops
- 1 tbsp ginger juice
- 3 tsp sugar
- 1/2 tsp salt
- 2 tbsp Japanese Sake
- 2 tbsp unsweetened soy sauce

Directions:

1. In a small bowl, mix the ginger juice with salt and 1 tsp sugar.
2. Rub the pork chops and leave them overnight to marinate.
3. In the morning, carefully put the chops into the vacuum bag and preheat your sous vide machine to 144 degrees F.
4. Seal the bag removing the air as much as possible, put it into the water bath and set the cooking time for 1 hour.
5. Mix 2 tsp sugar with sake and soy sauce and boil in a small skillet or saucepan until the sauce thickens a

bit.

6. Pour half of the sauce over the cooked pork chops and torch the glaze until it caramelizes.

7. Serve the chops over plain white rice, drizzling with the remaining liquid half of the sauce.

Nutrition per serving:

Calories: 236
Protein: 15 g
Fats: 14 g
Carbs: 9 g

Rosemary Pork

Time to prepare: 5 min
Time to cook: 1h 30 min
Servings: 2

You will need:

- 2 pork rib chops
- Salt and pepper to taste
- 1 tsp olive oil
- 2 rosemary sprigs

Directions:

1. In a small bowl, mix salt and pepper to taste.
2. Rub the pork chops and leave them overnight to marinate.
3. In the morning, carefully rub the marinated chops with olive oil, put them into the vacuum bag and preheat your sous vide machine to 144 degrees F.
4. Add the rosemary sprigs to the bag and seal it removing the air as much as possible, put it into the water bath and set the cooking time for 1 hour.
5. Serve the chops over plain white rice or mashed potatoes.

Nutrition per serving: Calories: 236
Protein: 15 g
Fats: 14 g
Carbs: 9 g

Roasted Garlic Pork Chops

Time to prepare: 5 min
Time to cook: 1h 10 min
Servings: 2

You will need:

- 2 pork rib chops
- Salt and pepper to taste
- 1 tsp olive oil
- 2 tbsp unsalted butter
- 2 garlic cloves
- 1 small onion,

finely chopped Directions:

1. In a small bowl, mix salt, pepper and the olive oil.
2. Rub the pork chops and put them into the vacuum bag.
3. Preheat your sous vide machine to 144 degrees F.
4. Add the garlic cloves and sliced onion to the bag and seal it removing the air as much as possible, put it into the water bath and set the cooking time for 1 hour.
5. Carefully dry the chops with the paper towels, removing the onion and garlic.
6. Heat 2 tbsp unsalted butter in a stainless steel skillet and roast the

chops on both sides for about 40
seconds (until light brown).

Nutrition per serving: Calories: 348
Protein: 30 g
Fats: 6 g

Carbs: 4 g

Pork Tenderloin with Shallots, Garlic and Herbs

Time to prepare: 5 min
Time to cook: 3 h 10 min
Servings: 4

You will need:

- 1 pound pork tenderloin
- 5-6 rosemary sprigs
- 2 garlic cloves, coarsely chopped
- 2 shallots
- 1 tbsp olive oil
- Salt and

pepper to taste

Directions:

1. Preheat the water bath to 150 degrees F.
2. Rub the pork with salt and pepper and put it into the vacuum bag.
3. Add a half of rosemary sprigs, 1 garlic clove, 1 shallot to the bag.
4. Seal the bag and cook in the preheated water bath for 3 hours.
5. When the time is up, carefully remove the pork from the bag and sear it on both sides over the high heat in 1 tbsp olive oil until light brown.
6. Quickly add the remaining 1

garlic clove, 1 shallot, 3
rosemary sprigs and sear for 10
more seconds on each side.

7. Slice the pork and serve with
mashed potatoes.

Nutrition per serving:
Calories: 236
Protein: 15 g

Fats: 14 g
Carbs: 9 g

BBQ Pork

Time to prepare: 5 min
Time to cook: 3 h 10 min
Servings: 4

You will need:

- 1 pound pork tenderloin
- 2 garlic cloves, coarsely chopped
- 2 tbsp garlic powder
- 2 tbsp ground paprika
- Salt and pepper to taste
- 1 tbsp dried oregano
- 1/2 tsp liquid smoke
- 1/4

cup BBQ sauce

Directions:

1. Preheat the water bath to 150 degrees F.
2. Mix salt, pepper, garlic powder, paprika and oregano in a bowl.
3. Rub the pork with the spice mixture and put it into the vacuum bag.
4. Add 1 garlic clove to the bag.
5. Seal the bag and cook in the preheated water bath for 3 hours.
6. When the time is up, carefully remove the pork from the bag

and sear it on both sides over the high heat in 1 tbsp olive oil until light brown.

7. Slice the pork and serve with the BBQ sauce.

Nutrition per serving:
Calories: 236
Protein: 15 g
Fats: 14 g
Carbs: 9 g

Chili Pork Chops

Time to prepare: 5 min
Time to cook: 1 h 10 min
Servings: 2

You will need:

- 2 pork rib chops
- 1 small onion, chopped
- 2 garlic cloves
- 2 tbsp Worcestershire sauce
- 1/2 tsp chili powder
- Salt and pepper to taste
- 1 tbsp unsalted butter
- 1

tbsp vegetable
oil Directions:

1. In a small bowl, mix salt, pepper and chili powder.
2. Rub the pork chops and put them into the vacuum bag.
3. Preheat your sous vide machine to 144 degrees F.
4. Add the garlic cloves, chopped onion, Worcestershire sauce and olive oil to the bag and seal it.
5. Set the cooking time for 1 hour.
6. When the time is up, carefully dry the chops with the paper towels.
7. Sear the chops in 1 tbsp butter on

both sides for about 40 seconds (until light brown).

Nutrition per serving:
Calories: 236
Protein: 15 g

Fats: 14 g
Carbs: 9 g

Sherry Braised Pork Ribs

Time to prepare: 10 min
Time to cook: 18 h + 10 min
Servings: 4

You will need:

- 2 pounds pork ribs, chopped into bone sections
- 1 tbsp ginger root, sliced
- 1/2 tsp ground nutmeg
- 2 tbsp soy sauce
- 1 tsp salt
- 1 tsp white sugar
- 1 anise star pod
- 1/4 cup dry sherry
- 1 tbsp butter Directions:

1. In a small bowl, combine salt, sugar and ground nutmeg, and rub the pork ribs with this mixture.
2. Put the ribs into the vacuum bag, add sliced ginger root, soy sauce, anise star and sherry wine.
3. Preheat your sous vide machine to 176 degrees F.
4. Set the cooking time for 18 hours.
5. When the time is up, carefully dry the ribs with the paper towels.
6. Sear the ribs in 1 tbsp butter on both sides for about 40 seconds

until crusty.

Nutrition per serving: Calories: 293

Protein: 12 g
Fats: 12 g
Carbs: 32 g

Beer Braised Pork Ribs

Time to prepare: 10 min
Time to cook: 18 h + 10 min
Servings: 4

You will need:

- 2 pounds pork ribs, chopped into bone sections
- 1 big onion, finely chopped
- 12 ounce can light beer
- Salt and pepper to taste
- 1 tbsp butter

Directions:

1. Rub the pork ribs with salt and pepper.
2. Put the ribs into the vacuum bag, add chopped onion and beer.
3. Preheat your sous vide machine to 176 degrees F.
4. Set the cooking time for 18 hours.
5. When the time is up, carefully dry the ribs with the paper towels.
6. Sear the ribs in 1 tbsp butter on both sides for about 40 seconds until crusty.
7. Serve with mashed potatoes, cole

slaw or white rice.

Nutrition per serving: Calories: 280
Protein: 20 g
Fats: 15 g
Carbs: 17 g

Chapter 12. Desserts

Cinnamon Apples
Time to prepare: 10 min
Time to cook: 1 h 10 min
Servings: **4**

You will need:

- 4 red apples, cored, peeled and sliced
- 4 tbsp butter
- 2 tsp ground cinnamon
- 2 tsp liquid honey
- Ju

ice of 1

lemon

Directions:

1. Set your cooking device to 180 degrees F.
2. Put the ingredients into the plastic bag, and seal it, removing the air.
3. Put the bag into the sous vide chamber and set the cooking time for 1 hour 10 minutes.
4. Serve warm in bowls with a spoon of vanilla ice cream (optionally).

Nutrition per serving: Calories: 250
Protein: 1 g
Fats: 12 g
Carbs: 35 g

Vanilla Pears

Time to prepare: 10 min
Time to cook: 1 h 10 min
Servings: 4

You will need:

- 4 pears apples, cored, peeled and sliced
- 4 tbsp butter
- 2

tsp liquid
honey

Directions:

1. Set your cooking device to 180 degrees F.
2. Put the ingredients into the plastic bag, and seal it, removing the air.
3. Put the bag into the sous vide chamber and set the cooking time for 1 hour 10 minutes.
4. Serve warm in bowls with

vanilla sauce.

Nutrition per serving:
Calories: 250
Protein: 1 g
Fats: 12 g
Carbs: 35 g

Lemon Curd

Time to prepare: 10 min
Time to cook: 1 h 10 min
Servings: 4

You will need:

- 1/2 cup white sugar
- 1/4 cup lemon juice
- 1 tbsp lemon zest
- 4 tbsp unsalted butter
- 1 1/2 tbsp gelatin
- 3 fresh eggs
- 1 tsp ground cinnamon

for sprinkling Directions:

1. Set your cooking device to 165 degrees F.
2. Put the ingredients into the plastic bag, and seal it, removing the air.
3. Set the timer for 1 hour.
4. When the time is up, blend the mixture with an immersion blender.
5. Wait until it cools down and refrigerates in portions.
6. Serve sprinkled with cinnamon.

Nutrition per serving:
Calories: 66
Protein: 1 g
Fats: 4 g

Almond Vanilla Pudding

Time to prepare: 10 min
Time to cook: 1 h 10 min
Servings: 4

You will need:

- 1/4 cup white sugar
- 1/4 cup vanilla sugar
- 1/4 cup almond milk
- 4 tbsp unsalted butter
- 1 1/2 tbsp gelatin
- 3 fresh eggs
- 1 tsp ground cinnamon

for sprinkling Directions:

1. Set your cooking device to 165 degrees F.
2. Put the ingredients into the plastic bag, and seal it, removing the air.
3. Set the timer for 1 hour.
4. When the time is up, blend the mixture with an immersion blender.
5. Wait until it cools down and refrigerates in portions.

Nutrition per serving: Calories: 159
Protein: 4 g
Fats: 4 g
Carbs: 28 g

Carbs: 12 g

Chocolate Pudding

Time to prepare: 10 min **Time to cook:** 1 h
Servings: 4

You will need:
- 1 cup milk
- 1 cup heavy cream
- 1/2 cup raw cocoa powder
- 1/4 cup lemon juice
- 3 fresh eggs
- 1/2 cup sugar Directions:
    1. Set your cooking device to 180 degrees F.
    2. Combine the ingredients and blend them with an immersion blender.
    3. Transfer the bag to the water bath and set the cooking time for 50 minutes.
    4. When the time is up, blend the mixture once with an immersion blender.
    5. Wait until it cools down and refrigerates in portions.

Nutrition per serving: Calories: 180
Protein: 4 g
Fats: 4 g
Carbs: 35 g

Pear & Lingberry Pie

Time to prepare: 10 min
Time to cook: 2 h 20 min
Servings: 4

You will need:

- 2 pounds sweet pears, cored, peeled and sliced
- 1/2 pound lingberries
- 3/4 cup sugar
- 2 tbsp cornstarch
- 2 tbsp butter
- 1 pack puff pastry
- 2 tbsp milk
- 2 tbsp sugar Directions:
    1. Set your cooking device to 160 degrees F.
    2. Put sliced pears, lingberries, cornstarch, sugar and butter in the vacuum bag and set the cooking time for 1 hour 30 minutes.
    3. When the time is up, cool down the filling to the room temperature.
    4. In the meantime, preheat the oven to 375 degrees F, grease a baking pan, and roll out 1 sheet of the pastry.
    5. Pour the filling over the sheet, and cover it with another sheet, seal the sheets on the edges with your fingers.
    6. Bake in the preheated oven

for 35 minutes.

Nutrition per serving:
Calories: 272
Protein: 3 g

Fats: 16 g
Carbs: 30 g

Apple & Cinnamon Pie

Time to prepare: 10 min
Time to cook: 2 h 20 min
Servings: 4

You will need:

- 2 pounds green, cored, peeled and sliced
- 3/4 cup sugar
- 2 tbsp cornstarch
- 2 tbsp butter
- 2 tsp ground cinnamon
- 1 pack puff pastry
- 2 tbsp milk
- 2

tbsp
sugar
Direction
s:

1. Preheat the water bath to 160 degrees F.
2. Put the sliced apples, cornstarch, sugar, cinnamon and butter in the vacuum bag and set the cooking time for 1 hour 30 minutes.
3. When the time is up, cool down the filling to the room temperature.
4. In the meantime, preheat the oven to 375 degrees F, grease a baking pan,

and roll out 1 sheet of the pastry.

5. Pour the filling over the sheet, and cover it with another sheet, seal the sheets on the edges with your fingers.

6. Bake in the preheated oven for 35 minutes. Nutrition per serving:

Calories: 272

Protein: 3 g

Fats: 16 g
Carbs: 30 g

Spicy Custard Crème

Time to prepare: 10 min
Time to cook: 1 h 30 min + overnight
Servings: 4

You will need:

- 2 cups heavy cream
- 1 cup milk
- 3 tsp ginger root, sliced
- 4 fresh egg yolks
- 1/2 cup brown sugar
- A

pinch of
salt

Directions:

1. Before preheating the water bath, arrange the ramekins: install the rack half-inch below the water surface.

2. Place 4 ramekins on the rack. Make sure the water level is not higher than 2/3 of the ramekins. Remove the ramekins and set aside.

3. Combine the heavy cream, milk and sliced ginger in a small saucepan and heat the mixture but do not bring it to boil. Cover the pan and set aside for 30 minutes.

4. In 30 minutes, strain the liquid, return it to the pan, and reheat again.
5. Whisk the egg yolks with salt and sugar, and carefully pour the cream mixture into the yolk mixture. Whisk well until even.
6. Pour the custards into the 4 ramekins, wrap them with plastic and return back on the rack.
7. Set the timer for 50 minutes.

8. When the time is up, cool the ramekins to the room temperature then refrigerate until cold and serve.

Nutrition per serving: Calories: 60
Protein: 0.7 g
Fats: 3 g
Carbs: 8 g

Crème Brulee

Time to prepare: 10 min
Time to cook: 2 h + overnight
Servings: 4

You will need:

- 2 cups heavy cream
- 1/2 tsp vanilla powder
- 1 cinnamon stick
- 4 fresh egg yolks
- 1/2 cup brown sugar
- A

pinch of
salt

Directions:

1. Install the rack in the water bath half-inch below the water surface.
2. Place 4 ramekins on the rack. Make sure the water level is not higher than 2/3 of the ramekins. Remove the ramekins and set aside.
3. Combine the heavy cream, vanilla powder and cinnamon stick in a small saucepan and heat the mixture but do not bring it to boil. Cover the pan and set aside for 10 minutes.
4. In 10 minutes, strain the cream and return it to the pan.

5. Whisk the egg yolks with salt and sugar, and carefully pour the cream mixture into the yolk mixture. Whisk well until even.
6. Pour the custards into the 4 ramekins, wrap them with plastic and return back to the rack.
7. Set the timer for 90 minutes.

8. When the time is up, cool the ramekins to the room temperature, then refrigerate until cold and serve.

Nutrition per serving: Calories: 60
Protein: 0.7 g
Fats: 3 g
Carbs: 8 g

Apricot and Cranberry Pie

Time to prepare: 10 min
Time to cook: 2 h 20 min
Servings: 4

You will need:

- 2 pounds ripe apricots, bone removed, halved
- 1/2 pound cranberries
- 3/4 cup sugar
- 2 tbsp cornstarch
- 2 tbsp butter
- 2 tsp ground cinnamon
- 1 pack puff pastry
- 2 tbsp milk
- 2

tbsp
sugar
Direction
s:

1. Preheat the water bath to 160 degrees F.
2. Put the apricots, cornstarch, cranberries, sugar, cinnamon and butter in the vacuum bag and set the cooking time for 1 hour 30 minutes.
3. When the time is up, cool down the filling to the room

temperature.

4. In the meantime, preheat the oven to 375 degrees F, grease a baking pan, and roll out 1 sheet of the pastry.

5. Pour the filling over the sheet, and cover it with another sheet, seal the sheets on the edges with your fingers.

6. Bake in the preheated oven for 35 minutes.

Nutrition per serving:
Calories: 272
Protein: 3 g
Fats: 16 g
Carbs: 30 g

Orange Yogurt

Time to prepare: 10 min
Time to cook: 3 h + 1 h
Servings: 4

You will need:

- 4 cups milk
- 1/2 cup greek yogurt
- 1 tbsp orange zest
- 1/2

tbsp lemon zest

Directions:

1. Pour the milk into a pan and heat it to 180 degrees F.
2. Cool it down to the room temperature.
3. Preheat the water bath to 113 degrees F.
4. Mix in the yogurt, add the orange and lemon zest and pour the mixture into canning jars.
5. Cover the jars with the lids and cook in the water bath for 3 hours.
6. When the time is up, cool down the jars to the room temperature and then refrigerate before serving.

Nutrition per serving: Calories: 120
Protein: 12 g
Fats: 3 g
Carbs: 6 g

Raspberry & Honey Yogurt

Time to prepare: 10 min
Time to cook: 3h + 1 h
Servings: 4

You will need:

- 4 cups milk
- 1/2 cup greek yogurt
- 1/2 cup fresh raspberries
- 2 tbsp honey Directions:

1. Pour the milk into a pan and heat it to 180 degrees F.
2. Cool it down to the room temperature.
3. Preheat the water bath to 113 degrees F.
4. Mix in the yogurt, add the raspberries, honey, and pour the mixture into canning jars.
5. Cover the jars with the lids and cook in the water bath for 3 hours.
6. When the time is up, cool down the jars to the room temperature and then refrigerate before serving.

Nutrition per serving: Calories: 140
Protein: 12 g
Fats: 3 g
Carbs: 17 g

Apple Yogurt with Raisins

Time to prepare: 10 min
Time to cook: 3 h + 1 h
Servings: 4

You will need:

- 4 cups milk
- 1/2 cup greek yogurt
- 1/2 cup sweet apples, peeled, cored and chopped into small pieces
- 1 tsp cinnamon
- 4 tsp small raisins
- 2 tbsp honey

Directions:

1. Pour the milk into a pan and heat it to 180 degrees F.
2. Cool it down to the room temperature.
3. Preheat the water bath to 113 degrees F.
4. Mix in the yogurt, add the apples, cinnamon, honey, raisins, and pour the mixture into canning jars.
5. Cover the jars with the lids and cook in the water bath for 3 hours.
6. When the time is up, cool down

the jars to the room temperature and then refrigerate before serving.

Nutrition per serving: Calories: 120
Protein: 12 g
Fats: 3 g
Carbs: 6 g

White Chocolate Mousse

Time to prepare: 10 min
Time to cook: 7 h + 24 h
Servings: 4

You will need:

- 2/3 cup white chocolate, chopped
- 1/2 cup milk
- 1/2 cup double cream
- 1/2 tsp gelatin powder
- 2 tbsp cold water

Directions:

1. Preheat your Sous Vide machine to 194 degrees F.
2. Place the chopped white chocolate in the vacuum bag.
3. Seal the bag, put it into the water bath and set the timer for 6 hours.
4. When the time is up, pour the chocolate into a bowl and stir with a spoon.
5. Pour the milk into a pan and warm it over medium heat.
6. Soak the gelatin powder in 2 tbsp cold water and dissolve it in the warm milk.
7. Carefully stir the milk-gelatin

mixture into the chocolate paste until even and refrigerate for 25 minutes.

8. Remove from the fridge, stir again and refrigerate for another 25 minutes.

9. Beat the cream to peaks and combine with white chocolate mixture.

10. Pour into single serve cups and refrigerate for 24 hours before serving.

Nutrition per serving: Calories: 218
Protein: 4 g
Fats: 15 g
Carbs: 19 g

Dark Chocolate Mousse

Time to prepare: 10 min
Time to cook: 7 h + 24 h
Servings: 4

You will need:

- 2/3 cup dark chocolate, chopped
- 1/2 cup milk
- 1/2 cup double cream
- 1/2 tsp gelatin powder
- 2

tbsp cold
water

Directions:

1. Preheat your Sous Vide machine to 194 degrees F.
2. Place the chopped dark chocolate in the vacuum bag.
3. Seal the bag, put it into the water bath and set the timer for 6 hours.
4. When the time is up, pour the chocolate into a bowl and stir with a spoon.
5. Pour the milk into a pan and warm it over medium heat.
6. Soak the gelatin powder in 2 tbsp cold water and dissolve it in the warm milk.
7. Carefully stir the milk-gelatin

mixture into the chocolate paste until even and refrigerate for 25 minutes.

8. Remove from the fridge, stir again and refrigerate for another 25 minutes.

9. Beat the cream to peaks and combine with white chocolate mixture.

10. Pour into single serve cups and refrigerate for 24 hours before serving.

Nutrition per serving: Calories: 218
Protein: 4 g
Fats: 15 g
Carbs: 19 g

Sous Vide Espresso Ice Cream

Preparation time: 2 hours
Cooking time: 20 minutes
Servings: 6

Ingredients:

- 5 egg yolks
- 3 tablespoons sugar
- 1 tablespoon instant espresso powder
- ½ cup water, hot
- 1 and ½ cup heavy cream

Directions:

1. In a blender, mix the egg yolks with the sugar, espresso powder, water and heavy cream, pulse well, pour this into a sous vide bag, seal, submerge in preheated water bath, cook at cook at 140 degrees F for 20 minutes, transfer to a container and freeze for 2 hours. Enjoy!

Nutrition: calories 202, fat 2, carbs 19, protein 7

Carrot Pudding

Preparation time: 10 minutes
Cooking time: 3 hours
Servings: 4

Ingredients:

- 3 tablespoons sugar
- 2 tablespoons almonds, chopped
- 2 pounds carrots, grated
- 1-quart milk
- 2 tablespoons raisins
- 2 tablespoons butter, melted

Directions:

1. In a sous vide bag, mix the carrots with the almonds, raisins and the butter, seal the bag, submerge in preheated water bath, cook at 183 degrees F for 2 hours and transfer to a pan.

2. Add the milk and the sugar, whisk, cook for a couple of minutes, divide into bowls and serve cold.

Enjoy!

Nutrition: calories 192, fat 4, carbs 11, protein 9

Strawberry Stew

Preparation time: 10 minutes
Cooking time: 20 minutes
Servings: 2
Ingredients:

- 2 cups strawberries, sliced
- 2 teaspoons sugar
- ¼ cup mulled wine

Directions:

1. In a sous vide bag, mix the strawberries with the sugar and wine, seal the bag, shake it, submerge in the preheated water bath, cook at 183 degrees F for 20 minutes, divide into bowls and serve.

Enjoy!

Nutrition: calories 205, fat 2, carbs 8, protein 4

Apple Stew

Preparation time: 10 minutes
Cooking time: 40 minutes
Servings: 4
Ingredients:

- 4 apples, peeled, cored and cubed
- 2 tablespoons butter, melted
- 1 tablespoon sugar
- ¼ teaspoon cinnamon powder

Directions:

1. In a sous vide bag, mix the apples with the sugar, butter and cinnamon, seal the bag, shake it, submerge in the preheated water bath, cook at 185 degrees F for 40 minutes, divide into ramekins and serve warm.

Enjoy!

Nutrition: calories 202, fat 4, carbs 14, protein 7

Espresso Pudding

Preparation time: 10 minutes
Cooking time: 20 minutes
Servings: 6
Ingredients:

- 6 egg yolks
- Sugar to the taste
- 1 and ½ tablespoons instant espresso powder
- 2 cups milk

Directions:

2. In bowl, mix the milk with egg yolks, sugar and espresso powder, whisk well, divide into ramekins, submerge them halfway through in your water bath, cook at 150 degrees F for 20 minutes and serve them cold. Enjoy!

Nutrition: calories 202, fat 2, fiber 1, carbs 14, protein 8

Easy Lemon Pudding

Preparation time: 10 minutes
Cooking time: 45 minutes
Servings: 4

Ingredients:

- 1 teaspoon butter, melted
- 2 egg yolks
- 3 tablespoons sugar
- ¼ cup lemon juice
- ½ tablespoon lemon zest, grated
- 1/3 cup milk
- ¼ cup flour

Directions:

1. In a bowl, mix egg yolks with sugar, lemon juice, lemon zest, milk and flour, whisk, divide into 4 ramekins greased with the butter, cover the ramekins with tin foil, place them in your water oven, fill it with water until it reaches halfway up the side of the ramekins, cook at 185 degrees F for 45 minutes and serve cold.

Enjoy!

Nutrition: calories 202, fat 3, carbs 11, protein 4

Chocolate Cream

Preparation time: 10 minutes
Cooking time: 30 minutes
Servings: 4

Ingredients:

- 1 cup heavy cream
- 1/3 cup milk
- 1 tablet dark chocolate, chopped
- 1 tablespoon sugar
- 3 egg yolks
- 2 teaspoons cocoa powder
- ¼ teaspoon vanilla extract

Directions:

1. Heat up a pan with the cream over medium heat, add milk, chocolate and stevia, stir until chocolate melts, transfer to a bowl, cool down a bit, add egg yolks, cocoa powder and vanilla and whisk.

2. Divide this into ramekins, put in your water oven, fill the oven with water halfway up the sides of the ramekins, cook at 180 degrees F for 30 minutes and serve cold.

Enjoy!

Nutrition: calories 200, fat 2, fiber 5, carbs 11, protein 7

Pear Stew

Preparation time: 10 minutes
Cooking time: 1 hour
Servings: 4

Ingredients:

- 2 cups mulled wine, hot
- 2 cups water, hot
- 1 cup maple syrup
- Sugar to the taste
- 4 pears, cored, peeled and cubed

Directions:

1. In a sous vide bag, combine pears with the water, wine, maple syrup and the sugar, seal the bag, shake, submerge in the preheated water bath, cook at 176 degrees F for 1 hour, divide everything into bowls and serve.
Enjoy!

Nutrition: calories 162, fat 3, carbs 9, protein 6

Rice Pudding

Preparation time: 10 minutes
Cooking time: 1 hour and 30 minutes
Servings: 4

Ingredients:

- 3 and ½ cups milk
- 1 and ½ cups rice
- ½ teaspoon cinnamon powder
- 1 tablespoon vanilla extract
- 1 tablespoon sugar

Directions:

1. In a sous vide bag, mix the rice with milk, vanilla and sugar, seal the bag, submerge in the preheated water bath, cook at 180 degrees F for 1 hour and 30 minutes, divide into bowls and serve with cinnamon sprinkled on top. Enjoy!

Nutrition: calories 202, fat 4, carbs 11, protein 7

Blueberry Stew

Preparation time: 10 minutes
Cooking time:
1 hour Servings: 8

Ingredients:

- ½ cup sugar
- 1 tablespoon lime zest, grated
- 1 tablespoon lime juice
- 1 pound blueberries

Directions:

1. In a sous vide bag, mix the blueberries with sugar, lime zest and lime juice, seal, submerge in preheated water bath, cook at 180 degrees F for 1 hour, divide into bowls and serve cold. Enjoy!

Nutrition: calories 132, fat 2, carbs 8, protein 5

Chapter 13. Rubs and Sauces

Bearnaise Sauce

Time to prepare: 10 min
Time to cook: 1 h
Servings: 10

You will need:

- 1/4 cup dry white wine
- ¼ cup white vine vinegar
- 1 tbsp scallion, chopped
- 2 tbsp tarragon, chopped
- 4 egg yolks
- 6 tbsp butter, melted
- Salt and

pepper to taste

Directions:

1. Set your cooking device to 174 degrees F.
2. In a large saucepan, combine the liquid, scallion and tarragon. Season the mixture with salt and pepper and simmer for about 5 minutes, until reduced twice.
3. Strain the liquid through a strainer and set aside.
4. In a bowl, whisk the egg yolks with the cooled mixture. Add the melted butter and mix well until

even.

5. Transfer the mixture to the vacuum bag, seal it and cook 45 minutes in the preheated water bath.

6. Blend the cooked sauce in a blender and serve with poultry.

Nutrition per serving: Calories: 38

Protein:2.4 g
Fats: 2.2 g
Carbs: 4 g

Jalapeno Sauce

Time to prepare: 10 min
Time to cook: 20 min
Servings: 10

You will need:

- 1 cup green jalapeno peppers, seeded and chopped
- 3 garlic cloves, minced
- ½ tsp salt
- 1/3 cup rice vinegar
- 4 tbsp simple syrup

Directions:

1. Set your cooking device to 99 degrees F.
2. Blend the peppers with garlic and salt with an immersion blender.
3. Carefully pour the mixture into the vacuum bag, seal and cook in the preheated water bath for 20 minutes.
4. Stir in the syrup and vinegar.
5. Serve with chicken, meat or fish – it works well with anything.

Nutrition per serving: Calories: 35
Protein: 0 g
Fats: 3 g
Carbs: 2 g

Hot Tomato Sauce

Time to prepare: 10 min
Time to cook: 20 min
Servings: 10

You will need:

- 1/2 cup hot red peppers, seeded and chopped
- 3 garlic cloves, minced
- ½ tsp salt
- 1/2 cup tomatoes in own juice, chopped
- 4

tbsp lime
juice

Directions:

1. Set your cooking device to 99 degrees F.
2. Blend the peppers with garlic and salt with an immersion blender.
3. Carefully pour the mixture into the vacuum bag, add the chopped tomatoes in own juice, seal the bag and cook in the preheated water bath for 20 minutes.
4. Stir in the lime juice.
5. Serve with chicken, meat or fish – it works well with anything.

Nutrition per serving: Calories: 43
Protein: 1.2 g
Fats: 1.2 g
Carbs: 6.8 g

Cheddar Cheese Sauce

Time to prepare: 10 min
Time to cook: 20 min
Servings: 5-6

You will need:
- 5 ounces Cheddar cheese, sliced
- 1/5 tsp sodium citrate
- 1/3 cup water Directions:
    1. Set your cooking device to 167 degrees F.
    2. Carefully place the ingredients into the vacuum bag, seal the bag and cook in the preheated water bath for 20 minutes.
    3. When the time is up, pour the sauce into a bowl and blend with an immersion blender until even.

Nutrition per serving: Calories: 80
Protein: 3 g
Fats: 5 g
Carbs: 4 g

Blue Cheese Sauce

Time to prepare: 10 min
Time to cook: 20 min
Servings: 5-6

You will need:

- 5 ounces blue cheese, crumbled
- 1/5 tsp sodium citrate
- 1/3 cup water Directions:
  1. Set your cooking device to 167 degrees F.
  2. Carefully place the ingredients into the vacuum bag, seal the bag and cook in the preheated water bath for 20 minutes.
  3. When the time is up, pour the sauce into a bowl and blend with an immersion blender until even.

Nutrition per serving: Calories: 73
Protein: 2 g
Fats: 6 g
Carbs: 2 g

Cranberry Sauce

Time to prepare: 10 min
Time to cook: 2 h
Servings: 5-6

You will need:

- 1 cup fresh cranberries
- Zest of 1/2 orange
- 7

tbsp white
sugar

Directions:

1. Set your cooking device to 194 degrees F.
2. Carefully place the ingredients into the vacuum bag, seal the bag and cook in the preheated water bath for 2 hours.
3. When the time is up, pour the sauce to a sauceboat and serve with lamb or beef.

Nutrition per serving: Calories: 54
Protein: 0.2 g
Fats: 0.4 g
Carbs: 14 g

Hollandaise Sauce

Time to prepare: 10 min
Time to cook: 40 min
Servings: 5-6

You will need:

- 1/5 cup white wine vinegar
- 2 shallots, finely chopped
- 1/2 cup butter
- 4 egg yolks
- 1/5 cup still water
- 1 tbsp lemon juice
- A

pinch of
salt

Directions:

1. Put the finely chopped shallots into a small saucepan, add the white wine vinegar and simmer until the liquid is reduced by half.
2. Set your cooking device to 185 degrees F.
3. Carefully pour the cooked shallots with the vinegar into the vacuum bag, add all other ingredients, seal the bag and cook in the preheated water bath for 30 minutes.

4. When the time is up, pour the sauce into a bowl, blend with an immersion blender and serve.

Nutrition per serving: Calories: 161
Protein: 2 g
Fats: 15 g
Carbs: 4.5 g

Thyme Garlic and Lemon Sous Vide Rub

Time to prepare: 10 min
Time to cook: 5 min
Servings: 2

You will need:

- 1 garlic clove
- 2 tbsp olive oil
- 1 tsp dried thyme
- 1 tbsp lemon juice
- Salt and pepper to taste

Directions:

1. Whisk all the ingredients in a small bowl.
2. Rub the mixture into the lamb leg or ribs and cook according to the instructions.
3. This rub is ideal for cooking lamb but can also be used for fish.
4. You can scale the amount of ingredients depending on the number of meat you are going to cook Sous Vide.

Nutrition per serving:
Calories: 120
Protein: 0 g
Fats: 14 g
Carbs: 0 g

Hot Cayenne & Mustard Sous Vide Rub

Time to prepare: 10 min
Time to cook: 5 min
Servings: 2
You will need:

- 2 garlic cloves, minced
- 1 tsp cayenne pepper
- 2 tsp mustard powder
- 2 tbsp olive oil
- 2 tbsp freshly ground black pepper
- 1 tsp salt
- 1 tsp onion powder

Directions:

1. Whisk all the ingredients in a small bowl.
2. Rub the mixture into the beef or pork and cook according to the instructions.
3. This rub is ideal for cooking pork and beef.
4. You can scale the number of ingredients depending on the amount of meat you are going to cook Sous Vide.

Nutrition per serving: Calories: 120
Protein: 0 g
Fats: 14 g
Carbs: 0 g

Paprika Sous Vide Rub

Time to prepare: 10 min
Time to cook: 5 min
Servings: 2

You will need:

- 2 garlic cloves, minced
- 1/3 cup ground paprika 1 tsp freshly ground black pepper
- 1 tsp chili powder
- 1 tsp onion powder
- 1 tsp salt Directions:

1. Mix all the ingredients in a small bowl.
2. Rub the mixture into the beef or pork and cook according to the instructions.
3. This rub is ideal for cooking pork and beef.
4. You can scale the number of ingredients depending on the amount of meat you are going to cook Sous Vide.

Nutrition per serving: Calories: 8
Protein: 0 g
Fats: 0 g
Carbs: 1 g

Easy Cranberry Sauce

Preparation time: 10 minutes
Cooking time: 2 hours
Servings: 4

Ingredients:

- 7 ounces fresh cranberries
- 2 tablespoons sugar
- Zest of ½ lime, grated

Directions:

1. In a sous vide bag, mix the cranberries with the sugar and lime zest, seal the bag,
submerge in preheated water bath, cook at 190 degrees F for 2 hours, transfer to a bowl,
blend using an immersion blender and serve. Enjoy!

Nutrition: calories 121, fat 2, carbs 11, protein 6

Famous Hollandaise Sauce

Preparation time: 10 minutes
Cooking time: 1 hour
Servings: 4
Ingredients:

- 2 tablespoons white vinegar
- 1 tablespoon shallots, chopped
- 6 ounces butter melted
- Salt and white pepper to the taste
- 3 egg yolks
- 2 tablespoons water
- 1 tablespoon lime juice

Directions:

1. Heat up a pan over medium heat, add shallots and the vinegar, stir, cook for 5 minutes and transfer to a bowl.
2. In another bowl, mix the butter with the egg yolks, salt, pepper, water, lime juice and the vinegar mix and whisk really well.
3. Pour this into a sous vide bag, seal, submerge in preheated water bath, cook at 180 degrees F for 25 minutes, then cook at 165 degrees F for 30 minutes more, divide into bowls and serve.

Enjoy!

Nutrition: calories 190, fat 4, fiber 8, carbs 13, protein 9

Jalapeno Sauce

Preparation time: 10 minutes
Cooking time: 20 minutes
Servings: 4

Ingredients:

- 1 pound red jalapeno peppers, roughly chopped
- 8 garlic cloves, minced
- Salt and white pepper to the taste
- 2 tablespoons balsamic vinegar
- 1 tablespoon simple syrup

Directions:

1. In a bowl, mix the jalapenos with the garlic, salt, pepper, vinegar and syrup, whisk, pour into a sous vide bag, seal, submerge in preheated water bath and cook at 190 degrees F for 20 minutes.

2. Transfer this to a blender, pulse, divide into bowls and serve.

Enjoy!

Nutrition: calories 121, fat 2, carbs 11, protein 6

Rich Mango Sauce

Preparation time: 10 minutes
Cooking time: 7 hours
Servings: 4
Ingredients:

- ½ pound mangos, peeled and cubed
- 2 tablespoons olive oil
- 1 teaspoon red chili flakes, crushed
- 1 tablespoon pineapple juice
- 1 tablespoon cider vinegar
- 2 tablespoons sugar
- 1 teaspoon curry powder
- Salt and white pepper to the taste
- 1 small red onion, minced
- 1 tablespoon ginger, grated
- 1 small red bell pepper, chopped

Directions:

1. In your blender, mix the mangos with the oil, chili flakes, pineapple juice, vinegar, sugar, curry powder, salt, pepper, onion, ginger and red pepper, pulse well, transfer to a sous vide bag, seal the bag, submerge in preheated water bath and cook at 180 degrees F for 7 hours.
2. Divide into bowls and serve cold.
Enjoy!
Nutrition: calories 149, fat 4, carbs 13, protein 6

Spiced Tomato and Cocoa Sauce

Preparation time: 10 minutes
Cooking time: 40 minutes
Servings: 4

Ingredients:

- 2 tablespoons canola oil
- 1 white onion, chopped
- 2 garlic cloves, minced
- 2 red chilies, minced
- 4 ounces tomato paste
- 2 tablespoons brown sugar
- 2 tablespoons cider vinegar
- 3 tablespoons cocoa powder
- A pinch of salt and white pepper
- 1 and ½ teaspoons cumin, ground
- 1 teaspoon coriander, ground
- 2 tablespoons lemon juice
- 1 tablespoon lime juice
- 1 tablespoon lemon zest, grated

Directions:

1. Heat up a pan with the oil over medium high heat, add the onion, garlic and the chilies, cook for 5 minutes and transfer to a bowl.

2. Add tomato paste, sugar, vinegar, cocoa, cumin, coriander, salt, pepper, lemon juice, lime juice and lemon zest, blend using an immersion blender, transfer to a sous vide

bag, seal, submerge in preheated water bath, cook at 170 degrees F for 40 minutes, divide into bowls and serve. Enjoy!

Nutrition: calories 191, fat 4, carbs 9, protein 5

Flavored Teriyaki Sauce

Preparation time: 10 minutes
Cooking time: 20 minutes
Servings: 4

Ingredients:

- 1 cup soy sauce
- ½ cup water
- ¾ cup sugar
- 1 tablespoon white vinegar
- 1 tablespoon canola oil
- 3 green onions, chopped
- 4 garlic cloves, minced

Directions:

1. In a bowl, mix the soy sauce with the water, sugar, vinegar, oil, garlic and green onions, whisk, pour into a sous vide bag, seal, submerge in preheated water bath, cook at 180 degrees F for 20 minutes, divide into jars and serve when needed.

Enjoy!

Nutrition: calories 150, fat 4, carbs 9, protein 5

Mint Sauce

Preparation time: 10 minutes
Cooking time: 2 hours
Servings: 3

Ingredients:

- Juice of ½ lime
- 1 and ½ cups mint leaves
- 1 teaspoon ginger piece, grated
- ¾ cup cilantro
- 1 tablespoon olive oil
- 1 tablespoon water
- Salt and black pepper to the taste
- 1 red chili pepper, chopped

Directions:

1. In your blender, mix the lime juice with mint, ginger, cilantro, oil, water, salt, pepper and Serrano pepper, pulse well, transfer to a ziplock bag, seal, shake, submerge in preheated water bath and cook at 130 degrees F for 2 hours.
2. Serve it warm with some chicken. Enjoy!

Nutrition: calories 130, fat 1, carbs 7, protein 4

Rosemary Lemon Sauce

Preparation time: 10 minutes
Cooking time: 20 minutes
Servings: 3

Ingredients:

- Juice of 3 lemons
- ¼ cup rosemary, chopped
- ¼ cup canola oil
- 2 garlic cloves, minced
- A pinch of salt and black pepper

Directions:

1. In a blender, mix lemon juice with rosemary, oil, garlic, salt and pepper, pulse a bit, pour into a sous vide bag, seal, submerge in preheated water bath, cook at 180 degrees F for 20 minutes, divide into bowls and serve. Enjoy!

Nutrition: calories 131, fat 4, carbs 9, protein 5

Pineapple and Soy Sauce

Preparation time: 10 minutes
Cooking time: 20 minutes
Servings: 4

Ingredients:

- 1 cup pineapple, peeled and crushed
- 1/3 cup soy sauce
- 1/3 cup honey
- ¼ cup cider vinegar
- 2 garlic cloves, minced
- 1 teaspoon ginger, grated

Directions:

1. In a blender, mix the pineapple with the soy sauce, honey, vinegar, garlic and ginger, pulse, pour into a sous vide bag, seal, submerge in preheated water bath, cook at 190 degrees F for 20 minutes, divide into bowls and serve as a sauce. Enjoy!

Nutrition: calories 100, fat 2, carbs 4, protein 6

Worcestershire Sauce Mix

Preparation time: 10 minutes
Cooking time: 30 minutes
Servings: 4
Ingredients:

- ¼ cup olive oil
- ¼ cup balsamic vinegar
- 2 tablespoons Worcestershire sauce
- Black pepper to the taste
- 2 teaspoons oregano, chopped
- ½ teaspoon thyme, chopped
- ¼ teaspoon onion powder
- 2 garlic cloves, minced

Directions:

1. In a bowl, mix the oil with the vinegar, Worcestershire sauce, black pepper, oregano, thyme, garlic and onion powder, whisk really well, pour into a sous vide bag, seal, submerge in preheated water bath cook at 180 degrees F for 30 minutes, divide into bowls and serve.

Enjoy!

Nutrition: calories 191, fat 4, carbs 10, protein 5

Chapter 14: Eggs

Coffee Shop Egg White Bites

Prep.time:10minutes
Cooking time: 1 hour
Serves: 6

Calories: 55, Fat 2.54 g, Carbohydrates 1.26 g, Protein 6.49 g

Ingredients:

- 6 egg whites
- ¼ cup plain Greek yogurt
- ½ cup feta cheese
- ⅛ teaspoon salt
- ¼ teaspoon pepper
- 2 tablespoons roasted red pepper, finely chopped
- 2 tablespoons fresh chives, finely chopped

Method:

1. Preheat the water bath to 172°F.
2. Beat egg whites, yogurt, cheese, salt, and pepper until smooth. Stir in red pepper and chives.
3. Pour the mixture into jars. Screw on lids finger- tight.

4. Cook for 1 hour. Carefully remove from water bath. Cool slightly before eating.

Deconstructed Quiche Lorraine

Prep.time: 30 minutes
Cooking time:30 minutes
Serves: 4

Calories: 316, Fat 24.78 g, Carbohydrates 7.66 g,
Protein 15.49 g

Ingredients:

- 3 large eggs
- 3 slices bacon, fried and chopped
- 4 ounces Gruyere cheese, shredded
- ½ cup plain Greek yogurt
- 2 tablespoons chopped fresh chives,
  plus extra for garnish
- Pinch nutmeg
- ½ teaspoon salt
- 1 teaspoon pepper
- 1 sheet refrigerated puff pastry

Method:

1. Use a biscuit cutter to cut the
   puff pastry into rounds. Bake
   according to package instructions
   until golden brown.
2. Preheat water bath to 165°F.

3. Beat eggs, then whisk in yogurt, chives, nutmeg, salt and pepper. Stir in bacon and cheese. Pour egg mixture into bag and seal using water

method. The egg mixture should collect in the bottom of the bag.

4. Place bag into bath. Cook for 20 minutes, then remove.

5. Gently remove the cooked egg to a cutting board. Using the same biscuit cutter that you used to cut the pastry, cut rounds from the egg. Place one round of egg on each pastry round. Sprinkle with chives.

Smoked Salmon Eggs Benedict

Prep time: 30 minutes
Cooking time: 2 hours
Serves: 4

Calories: 604, Fat 49 g, Carbohydrates 14.76 g,
Protein 26.15 g

Ingredients:

- 4 eggs
- 8 ounces smoked salmon
- 2 English muffins, split
- Sous Vide Hollandaise sauce, bagged and uncooked

Method:

1. Preheat the sous vide bath to 147°F.
2. Seal the eggs in a bag. Place the bag of eggs and the bag of hollandaise into the sous vide bath. Cook for 2 hours.
3. 30 minutes before the end of cooking time, toast and butter the English muffins.
4. Remove eggs and sauce from bath. Pour sauce into a blender and blend until smooth.

Meanwhile, cool eggs in a bowl of cold water.

5. Arrange 2 ounces of smoked salmon on each English muffin half to form a cup that will hold the poached egg. Carefully crack each egg over a slotted spoon held over a bowl to allow the excess white to drip away. Place one egg in each smoked salmon cup. Top with hollandaise sauce.

French Herb Omelette

Prep time: 10 minutes
Cooking time: 20 minutes
Serves: 1

Calories: 279, Fat 25.63 g, Carbohydrates 3.39 g, Protein 8.99 g

Ingredients:

- 3 large eggs
- 1 tablespoon unsalted butter, melted
- ¼ tablespoon fresh chives, minced
- ¼ tablespoon fresh parsley, minced, plus more for garnish
- ¼ tablespoon fresh tarragon, minced
- ¼ teaspoon fresh rosemary, minced
- 1 tablespoon plain Greek yogurt
- ¼ teaspoon salt
- ¼ teaspoon pepper

Method:

1. Preheat water bath to 165°F.
2. Beat eggs with butter and yogurt, then stir in herbs, salt, and pepper.
3. Pour eggs into bag and seal using the water method. Place

in water bath.

4. Cook eggs for 10 minutes, then remove and gently press the half-cooked eggs into an omelette shape. Replace in bath and cook 10 minutes more.

5. Gently remove omelette to plate.
   Garnish with parsley.

Simple Shakshuka

Prep
time: 10
minutes
Cooking
time: 2
hours
Serves:
3

Calories: 287, Fat 18.54 g, Carbohydrates 12.86
g, Protein
18.75 g

Ingredients:

- 1 28-ounces can whole peeled tomatoes, crushed
- 3 cloves garlic, minced
- ¼ teaspoon cayenne pepper
- 2 teaspoons ground cumin
- 1 tablespoon paprika
- ¼ teaspoon salt
- ¼ teaspoon pepper
- 6 eggs
- ¼ cup fresh cilantro, minced
- Crusty bread for serving

Method:

1. Preheat water bath to 147°F.
2. Combine tomatoes, garlic, cayenne, cumin, paprika, salt, and pepper in a bag. Seal using water method.
3. Place eggs in a separate bag. Seal using water method.

4. Place both sauce and eggs bags in the bath. Cook 2 hours.
5. Divide sauce between 3 bowls. Carefully shell eggs and place 2 in each bowl. Top with cilantro and serve with crusty bread.

Devilled Eggs Nicoise
Prep time: 30 minutes
Cooking time: 1 hour
Serves: 6

Calories: 160, Fat 12.38g, Carbohydrates 2.59 g, Protein 9.33 g

Ingredients:

- 6 eggs
- 2 tablespoons black olives, minced
- 1 small tomato, seeded and minced
- 1 teaspoon Dijon mustard
- Juice of 1 lemon
- 1 tablespoon olive oil
- 1 tablespoon plain Greek yogurt
- 2 tablespoons fresh parsley, minced, plus more for garnish

Method:

1. Preheat water bath to 170°F.
2. Place eggs in bag. Seal with water method, then place in bath. Cook for 1 hour.
3. Place eggs in a bowl of cold water to cool. Peel carefully,

then cut each egg in half
lengthwise.

4. Scoop egg yolks into a bowl. Stir
   in olives, tomato, mustard, lemon,
   oil, yogurt, and parsley.
5. Fill egg whites with the egg yolk
   mixture. Garnish with parsley.

Cheesy Grits & Eggs

Prep time: 20 minutes
Cooking time: 3 hours
Serves: 4

Calories: 444, Fat 28.47 g, Carbohydrates 21.02 g, Protein
25.23 g

Ingredients:

- 1 cup old-fashioned grits
- ½ cup plain Greek yogurt
- ½ cup milk
- 3 cups chicken stock
- 2 tablespoons butter, melted
- 4 ounces Cheddar cheese, grated, plus more for garnish
- 6 eggs

Method:

1. Preheat water bath to 180°F.
2. Whisk together grits, yogurt, milk, stock, butter, and cheese, then pour into bag and seal using water method.
3. Place in water bath and

cook 2 to 3 hours,
occasionally massaging to
prevent lumps.
4. When the grits have ½ hour left
to cook, place eggs in a bag and
add to water bath.

5. When the grits have absorbed most of the liquid, divide between 3 bowls. Carefully shell eggs and top each bowl with 2 eggs. Garnish with grated cheese.

Huevos Rancheros

Prep time: 30 minutes
Cooking time: 2 hours
Serves: 3

Calories: 554, Fat 34.66 g, Carbohydrates 32.71, g, Protein
28.57 g

Ingredients:

- ½ can (7 ounces) crushed tomatoes
- ½ small yellow onion, minced
- 2 cloves garlic, minced
- ¼ teaspoon dried oregano
- ¼ teaspoon ground cumin
- Juice of ½ lime
- 1 canned chipotle adobo chile, minced
- ½ can refried beans
- 6 eggs
- 6 corn tortillas
- ¼ cup fresh cilantro, chopped
- ½ cup crumbled cotija cheese or grated Monterey Jack

Method:
1. Preheat water bath to 147°F.
2. Combine tomatoes, onion, garlic,

oregano, cumin, lime, and chile in a bag. Seal using water method. Pour refried beans into a second bag and seal using water method. Place eggs into a third bag and seal using water method.

3. Place all three bags into the water bath. Cook for 2 hours.

4. When the other components have 20 minutes left to cook, heat tortillas in pan. Place 2 on each plate.

5. Top the tortillas with salsa, followed by the shelled eggs, cheese, and cilantro. Serve with refried bean

Bar-Style Pink Pickled Eggs

Prep time: 20 minutes
Cooking time: 2 hours
Serves: 6

Calories: 166, Fat 10.08 g, Carbohydrates 7.34 g, Protein 9.3 g

Ingredients:

- 6 eggs
- 1 cup white vinegar
- Juice from 1 can beets
- ¼ cup sugar
- ½ tablespoon salt
- 2 cloves garlic
- 1 tablespoon whole peppercorn
- 1 bay leaf

Method:

1. Preheat water bath to 170°F.
2. Place eggs in bag. Seal bag and place in bath. Cook 1 hour.
3. After 1 hour, place eggs in bowl of cold water to cool and carefully peel. In the bag in which you cooked the eggs, combine vinegar,

beet juice, sugar, salt, garlic, and
bay leaf.

4. Replace eggs in bag with pickling
   liquid. Replace in water bath and
   cook 1 additional hour.

5. After 1 hour, move eggs with
   pickling liquid to refrigerator. Allow
   to cool completely before eating.

Manhattan Pastrami Scramble

Prep time: 10 minutes
Cooking time: 15 minutes
Serves: 3

Calories: 287, Fat 21.28 g, Carbohydrates 12.76 g, Protein
11.38 g

Ingredients:

- 6 large eggs
- 2 tablespoons heavy cream
- 2 tablespoons butter, melted
- ½ cup shredded thick-cut pastrami
- ¼ teaspoon salt
- ½ teaspoon pepper
- 3 slices buttered rye toast for serving

Method:

1. Preheat the water bath to 167°F.
2. Whisk together eggs, cream, butter, and salt and pepper. Stir in pastrami.
3. Pour egg mixture into bag and seal using water method. Place in water bath and cook 15 minutes, gently

massaging every 3 to 5 minutes to form curds.

4. Serve pastrami scramble on rye toast.

Chapter 15: Sous Vide Side Dish

Sous Vide Asparagus Mix

Preparation time: 10 minutes
Cooking time: 15 minutes
Servings: 2

Ingredients:

- 1 large bunch of asparagus, trimmed
- 1 teaspoon red vinegar
- ¼ cup olive oil
- Salt and black pepper to the taste
- 1 tablespoon cilantro, chopped

Directions:

In a sous vide bag, mix the asparagus with the vinegar, oil, salt, pepper and the cilantro, seal the bag
Shake it well, submerge in preheated water bath Cook at 185 degrees F for 15 minutes
Divide between plates and serve as a side dish. Enjoy!

Nutrition: calories 171, fat 3, carbs 12, protein 6

Easy Okra Mix

Preparation time: 10 minutes
Cooking time: 30 minutes
Servings: 6

Ingredients:

- 1 pound cherry tomatoes, halved
- Salt and black pepper to the taste
- 1 yellow onion, cut into wedges
- 1 teaspoon olive oil
- 1 pound okra, sliced
- 1 small green bell peppers, cut into small wedges

Directions:

1. In a sous vide bag, mix the tomatoes with the salt, pepper, onion, oil, okra and bell peppers, seal, shake the bag, submerge in preheated water bath, cook at 180 degrees F for 30 minutes, divide between plates and serve as a side dish. Enjoy!

Nutrition: calories 150, fat 2, carbs 11, protein 7

Eggplant Salsa

This Mediterranean side dish is really tasty!
Preparation time: 10 minutes
Cooking time: 1 hour
Servings: 4

Ingredients:

- 1 eggplant, cubed
- 1 red onion, roughly chopped
- 1 teaspoon canola oil
- 1 tablespoon balsamic vinegar
- 1 tablespoon fresh oregano, chopped
- Salt and black pepper to the taste
- Zest of 1 lemon, grated

Directions:

1. In a sous vide bag, mix the eggplant with the onion, oil, vinegar, oregano, salt, pepper and the lemon zest, seal the bag, shake it, submerge in preheated water bath, cook at 180 degrees F for 40 minutes, divide between plates and serve as a side dish.

Enjoy!

Nutrition: calories 150, fat 3, fiber 2, carbs 9, protein 5

Broccoli and Tomatoes Mix

Preparation time: 10 minutes
Cooking time: 45 minutes
Servings: 6
Ingredients:

- 4 assorted broccoli heads, florets separated
- 12 cherry tomatoes, halved
- 10 black olives, pitted and sliced
- 6 tablespoons olive oil
- Salt and black pepper to the taste

Directions:

1. In a sous vide bag, mix the broccoli with the tomatoes, olives, olive oil, salt and pepper, seal the bag, shake it, submerge in preheated water bath, cook at 183 degrees F for 45 minutes, divide between plates and serve as a side dish. Enjoy!

Nutrition: calories 142, fat 4, carbs 11, protein 5

Beets and Radish Salad

Preparation time: 10 minutes
Cooking time: 1 hour
Servings: 4

Ingredients:

- 1 bunch red beets, trimmed, peeled and cut into wedges
- 1 bunch yellow beets, trimmed, peeled and cut into wedges
- 1 bunch radishes, trimmed and cut into wedges
- 10 ounces rocket leaves
- 2/3 cup walnuts, toasted
- 2 and ½ tablespoons balsamic vinegar
- 1 packet stevia
- Salt and black pepper to the taste
- 2/3 cup olive oil

Directions:

1. In a sous vide bag, mix the red and yellow beets with radishes, salt, pepper and half of the oil, toss, seal the bag, submerge in preheated water bath and cook at 180 degrees F for 1 hour.

2. Transfer the beets and the radishes to a bowl, add rocket leaves, walnuts, vinegar, stevia, salt, pepper and the rest of the oil, toss, divide between plates and serve as a side dish. Enjoy!

Nutrition: calories 168, fat 4, carbs 11, protein 5

Green Beans and Tangerine Sauté

Preparation time: 10 minutes
Cooking time: 1 hour
Servings: 4
Ingredients:

- 1 pound green beans, trimmed
- Salt and black pepper to the taste
- 2 ounces hazelnuts, toasted
- 2 tablespoons butter, melted
- Zest of 2 tangerines, grated
- Juice of 1 tangerine

Directions:

1. In a sous vide bag, mix the green beans with salt, pepper, hazelnuts, butter, tangerine zest and juice, seal the bag, shake it, submerge in preheated water bath, cook at 185 degrees F for 1 hour, divide between plates and serve as a side dish.
Enjoy!

Nutrition: calories 161, fat 2, carbs 8, protein 5

Coconut Squash Mix

Preparation time: 10 minutes
Cooking time: 1 hour and 10 minutes
Servings: 4

Ingredients:

- 2 tablespoons butter, melted
- A pinch of salt and black pepper
- 1 red onion, chopped
- 1 and ½ pounds summer squash, quartered and sliced
- ½ cup coconut milk

Directions:

1. In a sous vide bag, mix the butter with salt, pepper, onion, squash and milk, seal the bag, shake it well, submerge in preheated water bath, cook at 176 degrees F for 1 hour and 10 minutes, divide between plates and serve as a side dish. Enjoy!

Nutrition: calories 202, fat 3, carbs 15, protein 6

Italian Veggie Salad

Preparation time: 10 minutes
Cooking time: 2 hours
Servings: 6

Ingredients:

- 3 tomatoes, cut into chunks
- 3 zucchinis, cubed
- Salt and black pepper to the taste
- 10 garlic cloves, grated
- 1 red onion, roughly chopped
- 2 red bell peppers, roughly chopped
- 1 eggplant, cubed
- 4 tablespoons olive oil
- 5 basil springs, chopped

Directions:

1. In a sous vide bag, mix the tomatoes with zucchinis, salt, pepper, garlic, onion, bell peppers, eggplant, oil and basil, seal the bag, shake it, cook at 180 degrees F for 2 hours, divide between plates and serve as a side dish.

Enjoy!

Nutrition: calories 159, fat 3, fiber 4, carbs 11, protein 6

Cauliflower Mash

Preparation time: 10 minutes
Cooking time: 2 hours
Servings: 2

Ingredients:

- ¼ cup sour cream
- 1 cauliflower head, florets separated
- Salt and black pepper to the taste
- 1 tablespoon canola oil
- 2 tablespoons feta cheese, crumbled
- 2 tablespoons chives, chopped

Directions:

1. In a sous vide bag, mix the cauliflower with salt and pepper and the oil, seal the bag, submerge into preheated water oven and cook at 180 degrees F for 2 hours.
2. Transfer cauliflower florets to your blender, add sour cream, pulse well, add the cheese and the chives, toss well, divide between plates and serve as a side dish.
Enjoy!

Nutrition: calories 181, fat 4, carbs 16, protein 6

Mushroom Salad

Preparation time: 10 minutes
Cooking time: 1 hour
Servings: 4

Ingredients:

- 10 ounces spinach, torn
- Salt and black pepper to the taste
- 14 ounces mushrooms, chopped
- 2 garlic cloves, minced
- 2 tablespoons parsley, chopped
- 3 spring onions, chopped
- 4 tablespoons olive oil
- 2 tablespoons balsamic vinegar

Directions:

1. In a sous vide bag, mix the spinach with salt, pepper, mushrooms, garlic, onions, oil and vinegar, toss, seal the bag, submerge in preheated water bath and cook at 175 degrees F for 1 hour.
2. Divide between plates, sprinkle the parsley on top and serve as a side dish. Enjoy!

Nutrition: calories 140, fat 4, carbs 12, protein 7

Chapter 16: Cocktails & Infusions

Orange-Anise Bitters

Prep time: 10 minutes
Cooking time: 2 hours
Serves: 4

Calories: 140, Fat 0 g, Carbohydrates 0.06 g, Protein 0 g

Ingredients:

- The peel of one orange, pith removed
- 1 star anise
- 1 cup bourbon

Method:

1. Preheat water bath to 125°F.
2. Seal all ingredients into a bag and place in water bath. Cook 2 hours.
3. Strain bitters into a small bottle using a coffee filter or a cheesecloth. Before using in a cocktail, bring to room temperature.

Mulled Wine

Prep time: 10 minutes
Cooking time: 4 hours
Serves: 4

Calories: 269, Fat 0.13 g, Carbohydrates 33.74 g, Protein 0.57 g

Ingredients:

- 1 bottle red wine
- 1 cup hard apple cider
- ¼ cup honey
- 2 cinnamon sticks
- 3 star anise
- 5 whole cloves
- 1 orange, cut in half

Method:

1. Preheat water bath to 150°F.
2. Combine all ingredients in a bag and seal. Place in water bath and cook 2 to 4 hours.
3. Strain solids from wine using a coffee filter or cheesecloth. Serve hot.

Watermelon Mint Vodka Infusion

Prep time: 20 minutes
Cooking time: 2 hour
Serves: 4

Calories: 140, Fat 0.06 g, Carbohydrates 2.91 g,
Protein 0.23 g

Ingredients:

- 1 cup vodka
- 1 cup watermelon, cubed
- 2-3 sprigs fresh mint

Method:

1. Preheat water bath to 140°F.
2. Seal all ingredients into a bag. Place in water bath and cook 2 hours.
3. Strain solids from infusion. Use in your favorite martini recipe.

Peach Infused Bourbon

Prep time: 20 minutes
Cooking time: 2 hours
Serves: 8

Calories: 143, Fat 0.09 g, Carbohydrates 3.58 g,
Protein 0.34 g

Ingredients:

- 2 ripe peaches, cut into wedges, pit and peel removed
- 1 cinnamon stick
- 2 cups bourbon

Method:

1. Preheat water bath to 150°F.
2. Seal all ingredients into a bag. Place in water bath and cook 2 hours.
3. Strain solids from brandy using a cheesecloth or coffee filter. Bring to room temperature before using in cocktails.

Rummy Eggnog

Prep time: 30 minutes
Cooking time: 1 hour
Serves: 4

Calories: 551, Fat 35.54 g, Carbohydrates 27.42 g, Protein
14.03 g

Ingredients:

- 4 eggs
- 2 cups whole milk
- 1 cup heavy cream
- ½ tablespoon vanilla
- ¾ cup sugar
- 2 cinnamon sticks
- ½ cup rum
- Freshly-grated nutmeg for garnish

Method:

1. Preheat water bath to 140°F.
2. Beat eggs until pale and fluffy. Beat in milk, cream, vanilla, and sugar. Pour into bag with cinnamon stick and seal using water immersion method.
3. Place bag in water bath and cook 1

hour.

4. Strain solids from bag using a
   coffee filter or cheesecloth.
   Chill completely.

5. To serve, pour into glasses and top
   with freshly- grated nutmeg.

Lime-Ginger Gin Tonic

Prep time: 20 minutes
Cooking time: 2 hours
Serves: 4

Calories: 630, Fat 0.05 g, Carbohydrates 30.9 g,
Protein 0.22 g

Ingredients:

- 1 cup gin
- 1 lime, cut into wedges
- 1 inch ginger, peeled
- 1 ¼ cup tonic water
- 1 cup ice

Method:

1. Preheat water bath to 125°F.
2. Pour gin, ginger, and half the lime
   into a bag. Seal and place in water
   bath. Cook 2 hours. After 2 hours,
   remove to refrigerator and cool
   completely.
3. When gin infusion is cool, divide
   ice between 4 glasses. Strain
   solids from gin. Pour an equal
   amount of the gin infusion into
   each glass. Garnish with lime

wedge.

Mocha Coffee Liqueur

Prep time: 10 minutes
Cooking time: 24 hours
Serves: 8
Calories: 244, Fat 6.3 g, Carbohydrates 21.49 g,
Protein 1.74 g

Ingredients:

- 1 ½ cups vodka
- 1 pound coffee beans
- ½ cup cacao nibs
- 1 cup sugar
- 1 vanilla bean, split

Method:

1. Preheat sous vide to 150°F.
2. Combine all ingredients into a bag and seal. Place in water bath and cook 24 hours.
3. Strain solids from bag using a coffee filter or cheesecloth. Transfer to a bottle and bring to room temperature before using in your favorite cocktails.

"Barrel-Aged" Negroni

Prep time: 20 minutes
Cooking time: 24 hours
Serves: 4
Calories: 216, Fat 0.09 g,
Carbohydrates 17.3 g, Protein
0.07 g

Ingredients:

- ½ cup gin
- ½ cup vermouth
- ½ cup Campari
- ½ cup water
- 1 orange, cut into wedges
- ½ cup winemaking toasted oak chips

Method:

1. Preheat water bath to 120°F.
2. Combine all ingredients in a bag. Seal and place in water bath. Cook 24 hours.
3. Strain solids from liquid using a coffee filter or cheesecloth. Serve over ice.

Conclusion

Why is sous vide cooking such a popular cooking method these days? Why do people who try it end up loving this futuristic cooking style? Why do these recipes taste so good?

We are here to answer all these questions! So, let's get started. Find out everything about sous vide cooking and decide whether to try it or not. Sous vide cooking refers to cooking food in a controlled temperature environment and under vacuum. This means you have to put the food in a vacuum-sealed bag, then submerge it in a water bath and cook it at a very precise temperature.

This cooking method has gained a lot of fans all over the world over the last few years due to the fact that all the food cooked this method tastes way better. You can cook so many interesting and rich dishes using your water oven and we can assure you that they will all be really impressive. Once you get familiarized with this cooking method, you will really become a star in the kitchen! Sous vide dishes are textured, flavored, colored and so intense.

Now that you know why sous vide cooking is a new, healthy and an easy way to make wonderful dishes for friends, family and guests, will you try it? Be bold. Get a sous vide machine and start making some of the most special dishes of your life. In order to help you with this, we searched worldwide and discovered the best sous vide recipes. We gathered all these recipes in this next sous vide collection. Just check them all out.

Have fun and begin your new culinary experience right away! Make the best sous vide dishes today!

CPSIA information can be obtained
at www.ICGtesting.com
Printed in the USA
LVHW020113120521
687184LV00008B/1276